THE JESUS CONNECTION

To my grandson Daniel

THE JESUS CONNECTION

TO TRIUMPH OVER

ANTI-SEMITISM

• • •

Leonard C. Yaseen

CROSSROAD • NEW YORK

1985
The Crossroad Publishing Company
370 Lexington Avenue, New York, N.Y. 10017

Library of Congress Cataloging in Publication Data
Yaseen, Leonard C., 1912–
The Jesus connection.

1. Jesus Christ—Jewish interpretations.
2. Christianity and antisemitism. I. Title.
BM620.Y37   1985   296.3′872   85-6633
ISBN 0-8245-0718-5

CONTENTS

ACKNOWLEDGMENTS   vi
INTRODUCTIONS   vii
LETTER TO A CHRISTIAN FRIEND   1

1 • AN AWKWARD HISTORICAL FACT   3

2 • PRIOR SHOCK   9

3 • THE JESUS CONNECTION   16

4 • ONE GOD   20

5 • JESUS AND JUDAISM   25

6 • THE CRUCIFIXION   32

7 • CHRISTIANITY AND ANTI-SEMITISM   38

8 • ROME AND EARLY CHRISTIANITY   42

9 • BOOMERANG   47

10 • A REVERSAL OF DIRECTIONS   61

11 • BROTHERHOOD IN DEED   74

12 • DEFUSING DIFFERENCES   81

13 • THE JEWISH CONNECTION   85

Science and Medicine   88
In the Public Service   97 / *Film*   109
Television   119 / *Music*   128
Art   132 / *The Written Word*   136
EPILOGUE   144
LAST WORDS   146
PICTURE CREDITS   149
INDEX   151

ACKNOWLEDGMENTS

My gratitude to Kenneth Libo whose keen judgment and unstinting collaboration in editing as well as gathering source material for *The Jesus Connection* has been indispensable.

It has been my good fortune to have Rabbi Marc Tanenbaum as a long-time friend. His wisdom and guidance have made it possible for me to persevere in the resolution of seemingly contradictory religious viewpoints, past and present.

Special thanks to my dedicated secretary, Madge Dineen, for the endless typing of an ever-changing manuscript.

The Jesus Connection had the critical advantage of a Phi Beta Kappa English major, my wife, Helen.

INTRODUCTIONS

Few topics are of more crucial importance than the question of Jewish/Christian relations in the modern world. And the challenge is to overcome the intolerance, misunderstandings, and tensions that have often plagued Jewish/Christian relations in the past and to move toward a better understanding and mutual respect of each other's positions.

The reader knows that I write this as an evangelical Christian committed to the beliefs of the New Testament. No one expects me to be other than what I am. At the same time, those of us who are Christians must have sincere love and respect for those who share different convictions.

Let us not hide our differences under a basket. Let us follow the counsel of Martin Buber: Don't try to score points or defeat your partner in dialogue. Understand him or her; respect your partner's uniqueness; establish a warm relationship.

I have grown in my understanding of this since I made a personal commitment at the age of seventeen on a small farm south of Charlotte, North Carolina. It was as if I had met Jesus Christ face to face, a Jew born in Bethlehem and reared in Nazareth. I have walked with Him since then and have proclaimed His message on every continent of the globe.

It was that commitment to Christ that has made me deeply concerned about the social and personal evils of this generation. As a Southerner, I began to wrestle almost immediately in my conscience with the question of race. As soon as I began to study the Bible in earnest, I discovered the debt I owe to Israel, to Judaism, and to the Jewish people.

I realize that the record of the relations between Christians and Jews makes unpleasant and at times horrifying reading. The institutional church has sinned through much of its history and has much to answer for at the Judgment, especially for the anti-Semitism practiced against the Jewish people. I look also with sadness and deep regret at those episodes in history when Christians tried to "force" the conversion of Jews. To force men to believe is, I am convinced, against the will of God. Alcuin said to Charlemagne: "How can you force a man to believe what he does not believe? Faith is an affair of the will, not of compulsion." A Christian theologian, Tertullian wrote: "It is a fundamental human right, a privilege of nature, that every man should worship according to his own convictions." Others spoke in the same vein but their voices were barely heard above the thunder of the terrible intolerance and persecution in the Dark Ages of Christian and Jewish relationships.

Of course there have been some outstanding instances of Jewish/Christian cooperation and mutual assistance across the centuries, but on the whole the record has not been good.

A nineteenth-century French scholar once said: "I shall not try to write the history of intolerance. That would be to write the history of the world." He was correct!

However, there is one thing that all Christians and Jews must understand. It is equally as difficult to define a Christian as it is to define a Jew. One of the great questions in the world is "Who is a Jew?" An equally great question is "Who is a Christian?" Millions who profess Christianity could not possibly be true Christians in the biblical sense. For example, if a professing Christian is not dominated by love of neighbor, then he or she cannot possibly be called Christian. Thus many of the persecutions of history were caused by false Christians, who dragged the Name of their Master into the mire of bigotry, anti-Semitism, and prejudice.

I am an evangelical Christian who believes that God can be experienced in daily life and that we are known not only by the creeds we repeat but by the love we live out in our relations with our fellow men and women.

Evangelical Christians especially have an affinity for the Jews because the Bible they love is essentially a Jewish book written under the influence of God's Spirit. One theologian has said: "Remove the New Testament books written by the Jews and only two remain, Luke and Acts. Remove every Jewish concept, every Jewish influence from the New Testament and only a question here and there from a pagan source is left, scarcely enough for one short paragraph."

As for the Old Testament, no Christian can read it consistently without subscribing to a recent pope's statement: "Spiritually we are all Semites."

It is to the lasting glory of Judaism and Christianity that they have their roots in the Old and New Testament Scriptures, written so largely by Jews. No greater words have been penned than those of the Mosaic code and the Sermon on the Mount. As never before, the world needs to accept the ethical principles and follow the moral standards outlined in the Law of Moses and the sermons of Jesus. Through their application, social injustice and moral evil can be greatly reduced, if not eliminated. Dr. Abraham Katsh, past president of Dropsie University, and other scholars have demonstrated the close relationship between the Hebrew Scriptures and the foundations of American democracy. If the Holy Scriptures were proclaimed fearlessly and lived faithfully, our world could be changed for the better. There are theological differences that we may never agree on, but there are certain things we can work together for now that may make a better America.

Not everyone will agree with every conclusion of Leonard Yaseen's book, but it could be a contribution to the making of better Christians, better Jews, and a better America.

Billy Graham

I t is remarkable how little Christians and Jews know of one another. So, anyone like Leonard Yaseen who begins to build bridges across the gap of mutual ignorance and suspicion will have to return to their origins to recover those common threads with which we can hope to have a fresh, shared identity. His essay fits with all of our experiences: friendship bridges so many chasms created by mindless stereotypes. Prejudice—the habit of judging before we have a clear picture—is seldom really broached or exorcised by the mere fact that "some of our best friends are Jews." For those friends might justly feel, as Yaseen was often told, that we were making an exception for them!

We have to look again at history, especially at the "parting of the ways," to try to better understand what went wrong. There are, of course, various views on how to read the events surrounding and following the destruction of the Temple some forty years after the death of Jesus, and the witnesses often wrote from partisan viewpoints. Yet, the fact remains that the Jewish believers in Jesus became less and less welcome in the synagogue and were soon vastly outnumbered in the Christian ranks by converts from paganism. Moreover, some of the elements of conflict found their way into the Gospels themselves, where the new context sometimes turned what had been a "family feud" into an anti-Jewish polemic.

As a result, centuries of Christians have been taught to regard the Pharisees as bigots, and the Sabbath rest as a perverse form of legalism. That the Pharisees were champions of the cause of those same "little people" with whom Jesus spent his entire life can easily be lost on the ordinary reader of the Gospels. Nor will that same reader develop any feeling for the sense of wonder and delight which surrounds the recurrent celebration of God's gift of creation in the Sabbath release from work. Yaseen does not mention these two examples, but they leap out at Christians who have come to appreciate how Jewish their roots really are. Our Christian belief in the divinity of Jesus expressly affirms our recognition of his full humanity—as a Jew. The fact that this affirmation continues to be startling to many Christians underlines the need for a book like Yaseen's. Our faith in Jesus as the "One who was promised" would make us demur at the hypothesis of some historians (cited by Yaseen) that he had "no idea" of what would emerge from his mission, yet most contemporary theologians and historians realize that the radical break which led to the "parting of the ways" came in response to a concatenation of circumstances. Whether among these was a need not to offend the Roman Empire is eminently arguable, but certainly the conversion of people who had never encountered Judaism made it more and more difficult to continue together.

Yaseen's observations on the essential continuity of Christian with Jewish prayer and ritual are the most welcome of all. His inclusion of the "Our Father" is bold indeed, for I have often thought that we Christians and Jews could and should share this prayer together. While Christians would recognize a fresh accent of familiarity in Jesus' confident access to God as his Father, nonetheless the image of God as Father, as well as the recurrent themes in the prayer itself, are deeply imbedded in the Hebrew Scriptures. Perhaps one result of *The Jesus Connection* would be to allow our Jewish friends to step over centuries of mutual distrust, largely fomented by Christian attitudes of superiority, to share with us in public gatherings as we pray to our common Father: the God of Abraham, Isaac and Jacob, and Jesus.

Theodore M. Hesburgh, C.S.C.

The genius of Leonard Yaseen's book, *The Jesus Connection*, is that he has translated into everyday language and images some of the deepest wisdom that has emerged out of the 4,000-year historic experience of the Jewish people and of Judaism regarding the unity of the human family in the midst of its pluralism.

It is not widely known that there is a substantial body of Jewish doctrine and teaching which, though composed over the past four millennia, contains ideas, conceptual models, and spiritual and human values of surpassing insight and meaning for our present situation. Leonard Yaseen's compelling thesis regarding the possibilities of genuine reconciliation between Christians and Jews—and, ultimately, between all members of God's human family—is based on the Jewish doctrine of the nations of the world, which today we might well call the Jewish doctrine of pluralism and world community.

The relationship of the people of Israel to humankind takes as its first and foremost principle the fact that, according to the Torah, all men and women are descended from one father. All of them, not as races or nations, are brothers and sisters in Adam and are therefore all called *bene Adam*, descendants of Adam.

From the first century of the present era and thereafter, the "stranger within the gate" in ancient Palestine and in the diaspora who joined in the Jewish form of worship but without observing the ceremonial laws became known as a *yire adonay*, a God-fearer. A God-fearer was one who kept the Noachian principles, that is, the moral principles known to Noah and to pre-Israelite humanity. As described in the Babylonian Talmud, the seven commandments of the sons of Noah are these: the prohibition of idolatry, of blasphemy, of sexual immorality, of murder, of theft, of cruelty to ani-

mals, together with the positive commandments to establish courts of justice.

As Mr. Yaseen rightly declares, Jesus was steeped in this
Jewish tradition; his moral teachings and practices simply
cannot be understood apart from its rootedness in this Phar-
asaic tradition. Indeed, when St. Paul embarked on his mission to preach the Gospel in Asia Minor, his first converts
came from among "the God-fearers" who were attached to
the synagogues in Antioch, Ephesus, Corinth, Philippi, and
elsewhere in the diaspora. So profound were the linkages of
early Christianity with its mother faith of Judaism.

The great twelfth-century Jewish philosopher Maimonides formulated the normative Jewish conception, held to
and affirmed by all periods of Judaism, in these words:
"Whoever professes to obey the seven Noachian laws and
strives to keep them is classed with the righteous among
the nations and has a share in the world to come." Thus
every individual—Christian, Muslim, Buddhist, Hindu—
who lives by the principles of morality of Noah is set on a
par with the Jews. Indeed, a statement made by Rabbi Meir
(ca. 150 CE) is recorded three times in the Talmud: "The
pagan who concerns himself with the teaching of God is
like unto the High Priest of Israel."

Thus, this rabbinic doctrine about "the righteous among
the nations" who will be saved made it unnecessary, from
the point of view of the Synagogue, to convert them to
Judaism. At the same time, Jews pray daily in the Synagogue
for what appears to be the ultimate conversion of the gentiles not to the cult of Israel but rather to the God of Israel:
"Let all the inhabitants of the world perceive and know that
unto Thee every knee must bend and every tongue give
homage. Before Thee, O Lord our God, let them bow down
and worship, and unite Thy glorious name let them give
honor."

Thus, Judaism affirms that salvation exists outside the

Synagogue for all who are God-fearers, that is, all who affirm a transcendent reality as a source of meaning for human existence, and who also live by the moral code of the sons of Noah. Significantly, Maimonides affirms a special Jewish theology for Christianity (and Islam). He taught that Christianity and Islam are missionary arms of Judaism created by God to bring "the pagans and heathens of the world under the Lord's canopy."

These Jewish theological views therefore perceive and understand world pluralism as a positive good, and positive relations between Jews and Christians as a keystone of that global pluralism. Judaism thus advocates a unity of humanity which encourages diversity of cult and culture as a source of enrichment, and the conception of unity in the midst of diversity makes possible the building of human community without compromise of essential differences.

In this book, Leonard Yaseen recalls the noblest and highest values of both Judaism and Christianity. At their best and truest, both affirm belief in the fatherhood of God, the dignity of each human life created in the sacred image of God, common moral responsibility for the welfare of human society, accountability for the events of history, and shared obligation for ushering in the Kingdom of God. Both affirm commitments to a messianic age when we realize a change, a conversion, in the kind of life being lived on earth, and not just in the inner life of the individual. Wars and persecution must cease and justice and peace must reign for all mankind.

Grounded in this profound religious and moral tradition, Mr. Yaseen is rightly outraged by the continued manifestations of anti-Semitism, racism, hatred, bigotry, and verbal violence—all flagrant contradictions of the values and ideals which Christians and Jews profess to believe. How could the gospel of love have become a gospel of hatred? How could the people of the cross have made the Jews the cross among the peoples? Had Jesus lived today would not the "great hatred of anti-Semitism" have consigned that first century Jew to the crematoria of Auschwitz?

Unless and until those contradictions between professions and practices are faced and resolved in a decisive way, Mr. Yaseen avers, religion will not be able to evade the charges of hypocrisy. Pope John XXIII understood that profound moral challenge, and he is responsible for the Second Vatican Council's decisive rejection of anti-Semitism and all forms of religious and racial hatred. Leaders of world Protestantism understood that and provided guidelines for their communicants that rejected these historic hatreds and bigotries. Dr. Billy Graham and the Rev. Theodore M. Hesburgh, both my dear friends, and many hundreds of other Christian leaders have understood that and have led the way to a new era in Jewish-Christian relations based on mutual knowledge and reciprocal respect.

Leonard Yaseen stands four-square in the midst of this "new revolution of mutual esteem" between Christians and Jews.

Marc H. Tanenbaum

THE JESUS CONNECTION

LETTER TO A
CHRISTIAN FRIEND

Is enlightened coexistence possible between Christians
and Jews?

In discussing this question with Christian friends, we
have explored some of the reasons for age-old hostility and
attempted to separate fact from historic fantasy. In so doing,
we have become better and closer friends.

For years I had been disoriented by the history of Christianity and some of its excesses, for I could not reconcile
Church statements and deeds over the centuries with true
Christian values. As *The Jesus Connection* took shape, I
felt depressed and embittered by the martyrdom of countless people with whom I identified.

But with knowledge comes understanding. As I dared to
reach further, researching more deeply, studying our common heritage, I came to realize that anti-Semitism does *not*
represent true Christian values. That was not what Jesus
preached or condoned.

In my desire to improve relations between Christians and
Jews, I was faced with two glaring misconceptions. Christians have perceived Jesus as antithetical to Judaism. Jews
have viewed him as the cause of anti-Semitism.

In setting out to discover who Jesus really was, I found

1

that neither of these notions is valid. Contrary to certain long-held Christian beliefs, his life and teachings were utterly consistent with his Jewish upbringing and environment; Jews are wrong to consider Jesus the cause of anti-Semitism.

Jesus was a defender, not a denigrator, of Judaism. He loved his own people. I have been able to free myself of my own mental blocks concerning Christianity by focusing on Jesus' Jewish heritage. I have come to accept him as a towering teacher and moral guide; but this in no way compromises belief in his divinity. "Our Christian belief in the divinity of Jesus," observes Father Theodore Hesburgh, president of the University of Notre Dame, "expressly affirms our recognition of his full humanity—as a Jew."

My commitment to Judaism, in fact, has been reinforced through my search for the true Jesus. The friendship between Christians and Jews could be strengthened immeasurably if they were to retrace the path I have traveled in *The Jesus Connection.*

Leonard C. Yaseen

·1·

AN AWKWARD
HISTORICAL FACT

Little more than a decade from now all Christendom will celebrate a historic event—the two thousandth anniversary of the birth of Jesus. His life was tragically brief. His crucifixion alongside two common thieves was witnessed only by his mother, a handful of followers, and mocking Roman soldiers. Yet Jesus' death has profoundly influenced the course of history.

Missionaries for Jesus have traversed the globe; immense cathedrals have been constructed in his name; sculptures, paintings, and murals have been dedicated to his eternal glorification. The grim instrument of his execution, the cross, has been lovingly symbolized in gold, silver, stone, and wood reproductions.

Existence in an earlier, troubled world meant struggling without dignity or security, thus creating a fertile atmosphere for the spiritual comfort offered by the teachings of Jesus. The early conversion of many of his Jewish followers to Christianity was followed by the slow but relentless conquest of paganism. The new religion flourished. Today some 900 million Christians constitute powerful religious blocs dominating North and South America, Europe, Australia, and portions of Asia, Africa, and the Middle East.

As we approach the year 2000, many denominations devoted to Jesus worship him in separate ways, leading frequently to bitter dissension. But one all-pervasive attitude persists among individual Christians of every denomination, and that is the denigration of Jews—the denial of their vocation and destiny in God's plan. This attitude lives on despite official ecclesiastical denunciation of anti-Semitism.

In the fourth century, Church Father Saint John Chrysostom laid the foundation for succeeding generations of the teaching of contempt: "Are [Jews] not inveterate murderers, destroyers, men possessed by the devil—debauchery and drunkenness have given them the manners of the pig and lusty goat. They know only one thing, to satisfy their gullets, get drunk, and maim one another. . . . Indeed they have surpassed the ferocity of wild beasts for they murder their offspring and immolate them to the devil. The synagogue? . . . a house of prostitution, a caravan of brigands, a repair of wild beasts, the domicile of the devil, an assembly of criminals."

Sixteen hundred years later Hitler inflamed latent anti-Semitism, claiming in *Mein Kampf:* "The personification of the devil as a symbol of evil assumes the living shape of the Jew. . . . He lowers the racial level by poisoning individuals. . . . In politics he replaces the idea of democracy by dictatorship. . . . The German intelligentsia no longer offers any resistance to the Jewish disease, syphilis."

Would intelligent people in the twentieth century believe this claptrap? They would and did—blindly. The followers of Hitler helped him systematically slaughter one half of the world's Jews.

How could this have happened—and why? Bluntly stated, many Christians through the centuries have loved Jesus but illogically, on the basis of early religious instruction, they have been taught to set him apart from his people. This policy of prejudice results in rejection, rejection brings exclusion, and exclusion confers a sense of superiority to extremists of any religion that can end in ghettoizing, violence, and genocide.

Jesus loved his fellow Jews. There were no Christians then. As a teacher, a Pharisee who adhered strictly to Jewish tradition, he would have been horrified to learn that his death would cause centuries of degradation and destruction of his coreligionists.

The passage of time, the shadows cast by conflicting accounts, and the intense emotions that shaped distortions of actual events have led to a major misconception of how close Jews were to Jesus. Many otherwise well-intentioned Christians still hold "the Jews" culpable for the death of Jesus. And included in their list of perpetrators are Jewish children playing baseball with other kids two thousand years after the fact.

This archaic Christian message makes it all but impossible for Jews today to continue to accept Jesus as one of their greatest teachers. In their despair, many have erroneously equated Jesus with extreme elements within Christianity responsible for their humiliation, persecution, and near annihilation.

I have devoted considerable time to investigating our common roots in order to better understand the paradoxical relationship that now exists between Christians and Jews. For years I was unable to see beyond my own experiences. But now, after a painstaking period of researching and rethinking prior assumptions, I realize how events purported to have happened in the past could easily have caused misunderstandings between our separate faiths.

For this reason alone, it is important that we arrive at some agreement regarding Jesus and his relationship to Jews. From the New Testament and from many other sources it can be reasonably assumed that:

- Ancient Israel was surrounded by pagan nations. The unique concepts of one God and man as made in His image paved the way for Christianity.

- In Jesus' time, there were diverse sects within Judaism just as there are today in Christianity. When Jesus was critical of certain attitudes, he was no more anti-Jewish than Luther or Calvin were anti-Christian in their criticism of Catholicism.

- Some Jews in the time of Jesus, far from calling for his death, revered him as their Messiah.

- As long as he lived, Jesus symbolized for a desperate minority a hope of throwing off the oppressive weight of Roman tyranny.

- Because his charismatic hold on Jews posed a threat to Rome, Jesus was crucified not by Jews but by Caesar's representatives.

- Jesus died not as a Christian but the way he lived, as a Jew.

- Early Christianity was a Jewish sect and remained so for decades, until a new religion was created, one that espoused an attitude toward Jews unknown to Jesus.

- Some statements expressed in the Gospels, three of which were compiled by Jews (Mark, Matthew, and John), have been misinterpreted, leading to Christian anti-Semitism.

Anti-Semitism is the end result of centuries of programmed prejudice by those who have preached love but practiced hate to the point of knowingly violating the most revered principles of their faith. Many Christians consciously disassociate themselves emotionally and intellectually from anything that strikes them as particularly Jewish.

It is a difficult attitude to control because of the cumulative effects of anti-Semitism—both overt and subtle—expressed in churches and clubs, business and social situations, practically every facet of some people's lives.

The Jesus Connection is devoted to the all-important task of providing new dimensions that could alter this way of thinking. The Jewishness of Jesus is "an awkward historical fact," according to John Haynes Holmes, "that the ordinary Christian so dislikes to remember" because it reminds him of the painful incongruity of revering Christ but despising and obscuring his origins. It is important to be reminded that Jesus was born into Judaism, was inspired by the teachings of Israel, and offered his message to humanity. To use him as an instrument of hatred against his own people is incomprehensible.

Some Christians say: "Jews are a people apart—they simply don't figure in my life." It's a thought commonly expressed, but inaccurate. In the everyday, real world, people *do* identify with Jews. When they use digitalis, insulin, streptomycin, polio vaccine, or draw plasma from a blood bank, read a book by Theodore White, Leon Uris, or Saul Bellow, watch performers like Jack Lemmon, Kirk Douglas, Goldie Hawn, Paul Newman, Shatner and Nimoy of *Star Trek*, Michael Landon and Lorne Greene, or recognize the contributions of Einstein, Freud, Cardozo, and Brandeis. Their profiles in this book serve as a reminder of the absurdity of anti-Semitism.

No Jew living today has escaped the destructive impact of bigotry, which has colored interreligious relations for nearly two thousand years. I am no exception. The far-reaching events of that unrelenting past have left their imprint on me.

Only recently, while working on this manuscript on a flight to California, a man seated next to me inquired, "What are you toiling away on?" At the time, I was transcribing a passage from the New Testament.

"I'm doing a study on the Jewishness of Jesus," I replied.

"That's a very Christian thing to do," he commented, and we carried on a pleasant and stimulating conversation over lunch.

A little later, he confided, "Considering everything we know about them, isn't it hard to believe Jesus was a Jew?"

"Not for me," I replied. "I'm also writing about anti-Semitism." He looked surprised and turned away. Some time elapsed before he asked, "Are you Jewish?"

"Yes," I replied and turned back to reading the Gospels.

That was the end of our exchange. A barrier now separated us, impenetrable as a stone wall. I no longer "belonged" in his world.

How can I describe how it feels to be accepted as a fellow human being one minute and then suddenly, for no good reason, to be ignored and dismissed?

Because there is no better way of revealing the ugliness of anti-Semitism than through personal experience, the brief chapter that follows is autobiographical in nature.

·2·

PRIOR SHOCK

The snowballs were packed with rocks. Barely ten years old, I was being assaulted for some mysterious reason. One assailant was a school friend with whom I had shared my lunch the previous day. What had I done since yesterday?

Minor harassments became part of my daily existence—frequent scuffles prompted by something far more threatening than youthful exuberance. Even at this early age, I felt the pain of self-doubt, uncertainty, and disillusionment.

All this took place many years ago in a small town in Illinois where my father, a Texan by birth, had been president of the Chamber of Commerce and, as far as I know, the only non-Christian ever invited to join the local country club. He reluctantly refused, paraphrasing Bernard Baruch: "Are you changing your bylaws or making an exception of me?" A thousand people came to my father's funeral to show their appreciation for his civic contributions.

Perhaps it was because of my father's influence that I believed fervently the words of the Pledge of Allegiance, that we were "one nation (under God) indivisible with liberty and justice for all." I am confident that many of my schoolmates shared my sentiments; but though they could live comfortably within the framework of that principle, it didn't quite work that way for me.

As my classmates grew older, they learned to express their prejudices more discreetly. In high school I took this as a sign of improved conditions. Indeed, an extraordinary event occurred in my senior year: I was elected mayor of our midwestern school by two thousand fellow students.

Soon after the election, Principal Boyer invited me into his office, to receive his personal congratulations I assumed. But instead he announced, "Leonard, you did receive more votes than any of the other five candidates; however, the faculty has decided that there will be a runoff between you and the next candidate."

Despite the passage of half a century, the memory of that moment remains frighteningly clear. Stunned and outraged, I managed to blurt out, "Has this ever been done before?"

"No."

"Then why are you changing the rules now?"

His silence seemed an ominous admission that some kind of conspiratorial decision had been reached that could not bear rational discussion.

A new election was arranged for several weeks later. During the interim one could not help noting feverish activities, surreptitious comings and goings, and what seemed to me a lot of unwarranted agitation in the office of administration.

I lost that second election by some thirty or forty votes to my closest contender, someone I had always admired.

Another blow struck at almost the same time. I had fallen in love with a wonderful girl, whose parents, though voicing no objection to me personally, insisted we stop seeing each other because of our different faiths. We fought an extended battle, but in the end had to capitulate to her parents' demands. I will never forget the day we agreed to separate. I was seventeen and didn't know how to respond to her parents' ultimatum. There was no way for me to comprehend their acceptance of me as their daughter's friend, but not as her suitor.

Francis Bacon observed that "the virtue of adversity is fortitude." Perhaps, but coping with these events while still in my teens was psychologically debilitating. I longed to enter a larger world where I could escape the burden of small-town bigotry.

In this frame of mind I left for college with no resentment toward my classmates, many of whom remained friends in later years. I was perplexed, however, by their parents, some of whom were a part of a prejudiced "establishment" whose capacity for social discrimination shocked me. Given the contradictory nature of the human condition, it is hardly surprising that these were the very same kind, gentle neighbors who never failed to stop and chat, who brought food into our home when my mother was ill, and who wrote considerate letters when an important event occurred in our family.

Entering the University of Illinois with high hopes, I was totally unprepared for the degree to which firmly established religious views dictated the actions of my fellow underclassmen. Though the university was multiethnic, it was no melting pot. Instead, there were a number of exclusionary cliques formed along religious and ethnic lines.

Seeking companionship, I joined a Jewish fraternity. This cut me off completely from any chance of social interaction with those of different faiths, for it was a long-standing policy of fraternities and sororities that there was to be no socializing between Christians and Jews.

A window to the outside world was opened for our somewhat provincial student body when famous artists performed at the university's huge auditorium in the spring. Vladimir Horowitz was scheduled to appear in May and we were selected as the host fraternity for the duration of his visit.

I was overwhelmed at the prospect of being so close to the world's greatest pianist. It was the middle of the depression and I was earning my tuition by also playing the piano—badly.

Horowitz arrived, dined with us, and then performed magnificently before a huge, appreciative university audience. Returning afterward, he consented to play our grand piano. When he rendered his own arrangement of "Tea for Two," I was fascinated, not only with his technique, but also the power and grace of his slender hands.

Horowitz's presence got me thinking. Here was a Jew treated with the greatest of deference by the very same people who, in their daily lives, practiced prejudice. I could not help but wonder if tolerance is extended only to superstars.

During my years at the University of Illinois, there were times of great inspiration, such as Horowitz's visit, professors whose classes I enjoyed, athletic activities that were exhilarating. But there was still no deep-seated happiness or fulfillment as long as I found myself between two worlds, one inhabited by people who reminded me of many of my friends back home, the other—the world of my fraternity—friendly but unfamiliar. These years left a residue of uncertainty and a need for understanding.

Much later, as the founder of a New York consulting firm specializing in industrial economic geography, I came in contact with business leaders from all over the world. Since neither my appearance nor my name are particularly "Jewish," there was ample opportunity to overhear indiscreet remarks aimed at others from time to time.

It was as if a part of me was invisible. A number of times I questioned my clients. Their responses became all too predictable: "Oh, Leonard. We didn't mean *you!*"

I hardly expected to belong to my clients' social and athletic clubs, let alone the yacht club adjoining the home I've lived in for thirty-two years, though I am a guest from time to time. But when attending dinner parties at private clubs with acquaintances of long standing, I have noticed Japanese, German, Italian, and other European and Asiatic executive transferees to our community. These people have become new members, but neither I, a fourth-generation American, nor any other Jew has been invited to join.

My consulting organization expanded rapidly. As a representative of many giant conglomerates, I traveled to South America, Europe, Asia; and wherever I went was accepted as an American, even in Arab countries. With international recognition came the merger of my company into one of the nation's most prestigious corporations. Throughout the time I was working with top management, I was treated with honesty, appreciation, and courtesy, yet there was no place for me as an executive *within* the corporation.

Possessing the symbols of success, I am considered successful. Then why should I complain about discriminatory practices? Nothing that has happened to me or my family thus far could be construed as life threatening. We haven't faced extermination in gas ovens. We weren't shipped off to Russian labor camps or threatened with annihilation by Arab terrorists, though we might have been were it not for an accident of geography and the determination of American leaders like George Washington, who wrote in 1790 to the Jewish congregation of Newport, Rhode Island, "Happy the government of the United States, which gives to bigotry no sanction, to persecution no assistance, requires only that they who live under its protection should demean themselves as good citizens in giving it on all occasions their effectual support."

Thomas Jefferson proposed a seal for the United States portraying the Jews crossing the Red Sea pursued by the Egyptians with the motto "Rebellion to tyrants is obedience to God."

A verse from the Old Testament, Leviticus 25:10, is engraved on the Liberty Bell in Philadelphia: "Proclaim liberty throughout the land, unto all the inhabitants thereof."

Roger Williams, the founder of Rhode Island, believed government should not be involved in religion but with matters of crime and law. The state charter decrees that no one should be "in any wise molested, punished, disquieted . . . for a difference of opinion in matters of religion."

A logical outgrowth of these liberal sentiments is contained in the belief that a mosaic of differing cultures works best in an open society. With principles such as these to guide us, we have achieved moral and social gains virtually unmatched in the rest of the world.

Yet even in America it is not easy for me to dismiss lightly the seemingly minor acts of rejection that have been a part of my life. On the surface they appear innocuous, but a closer look reveals a recurring motif of religious intolerance. First, the classical oratory of prejudice: "You don't belong." Then the rhetoric of exclusion, which relegates outsiders to an inferior position with the pronouncement that salvation exists only within the church for those who have seen the light. What results is a clear dividing line, a "wall of truth" separating Christians from non-Christians.

"This radical distinction influences the way Christians interpreted their life in society, their personal associations and their political ideals. It served as the key for an understanding of history," observed the Reverend John T. Pawlikowski, O.S.M., of the Catholic Theological Union of Chicago.

Identifying this viewpoint as an obstruction to religious fellowship, he continues, "*We* hold the truth, *they* the error. We have access to salvation; they sit in darkness and are filled with fear. We are virtuous, understanding, liberated, cultured; they are treacherous, fanatical, uncivilized. This deep division between 'we' and 'they' inevitably generates a sense of superiority. We are superior; they are inferior." Once a person is stamped inferior, he can then be assigned to the scrap heap (like a factory reject) without guilt.

Attitudes such as these made it all the easier for Klaus Barbie, the infamous "Butcher of Lyon," to deport forty-one innocent Jewish orphans, aged three to thirteen, from France to the gas ovens at Auschwitz.

The perpetuation of our form of government is contingent on our ability to prevent future Klaus Barbies from destroying our freedoms. As long as this potential threat exists, democracy is jeopardized whenever prejudicial distinctions are made against fellow Americans. Because such actions are so dangerous to our basic values, we must learn to repudiate them.

Christians might begin by reminding themselves that Jesus was a dedicated Jew who looked upon his people and their shared traditions with love and admiration.

·3·

THE JESUS CONNECTION

L et us close our eyes and imagine how Jesus might
have appeared to his followers. If what comes to mind
is a strapping young man, tall in stature, with Nordic features, there is reason to believe we are mistaken. For, by
modern standards, Jesus was, in all likelihood, small and
slender with penetrating dark eyes, a swarthy complexion,
and prominent Semitic features. His hair was probably
shoulder length.

Though no one knows the actual physical appearance of
Jesus, his image emerges for the first time in the ancient
Roman catacombs, where he resembles a bearded Orthodox
Jew. This is undoubtedly a close likeness, for Jesus was an
Israelite of his time and place.

Jesus of Nazareth was of the tribe of Judah linked to
David, Abraham, and Moses. A Jewish mother, Mary, nursed
him. A Jewish father, Joseph, taught him a carpenter's skills.
He spent his entire life among Jews and learned the Psalms
of David and the Law of Moses. The language he spoke was
Aramaic, the language spoken by Jews at the time.

Laborers, fishermen, tax collectors, prostitutes, and other
social outcasts were his friends. But despite these humble
beginnings he became known as a great teacher. Tales of
his mysterious powers followed him in his travels throughout the land.

Jesus grew up in a typical Jewish family environment, the first of several children. This is made quite explicit in Matthew: ". . . he [Joseph] took his wife [Mary], but knew her not *until* she had borne a son" (1:24–25). And: "Is not this the carpenter's son? Is not his mother called Mary? And are not his brothers James and Joseph and Simon and Judas? And are not all his sisters with us? . . . But Jesus said to them 'A prophet is not without honor except in his own country and in his own house' " (13:55–57).*

The Gospel of Luke tells of Jesus, at the age of twelve, being taken by his parents to Jerusalem at Passover. Jesus disappeared and could not be found. "After three days they found him in the temple, sitting among the teachers, listening to them and asking them questions; and all who heard him were amazed at his understanding and his answers" (2:46–47). Jesus was preparing for his bar mitzvah, a ritual that provides induction into Judaism at the age of thirteen for "one (who) is responsible for obedience to the Commandments."

Will you join me in exploring how and why an obscure teacher who lived two thousand years ago could have inspired so much love—and through no fault of his, despair—for so many centuries?

* * * * *

Never has one being, before or since, been the focus of passions that have altered the course of history, changed international boundaries, and so thoroughly possessed the souls of men and women. Never has anyone been so glorified, received such homage, adulation, and reverence.

The name of Jesus is on the lips of millions upon millions

---

*It should be noted that here and in similar references Catholic tradition regards the "brothers" and "sisters" of Jesus as relatives but not siblings. Likewise, according to Catholic teaching, the Semitic idiom in the use of the word *until* does not imply that Joseph and Mary had conjugal relations after the birth of Jesus.

of believers as they rise in the morning and retire at night. For many, life itself would be devoid of purpose and meaning without the comfort of Jesus.

When one realizes the total impact of his life and deeds, there is no need to be told how vital Jesus is to Christian beliefs. I wonder, though, if Christians realize how significant Jesus has also been to people of the Jewish faith.

Whatever one's religion, few can remain untouched by Jesus' compassionate teachings. Yet the religion founded in his name ignores his philosophy of love by debasing the Jews—his own people, his earliest followers. For centuries they have been viewed by the Church as culpable for their alleged role in his crucifixion, though, in fact, Jews were among Jesus' most ardent supporters. His immediate followers considered themselves the most fortunate of Jews. They could participate in all Temple rites, never questioning their Jewishness; in addition, Jesus, their rabbi, was considered a messiah. The news of his resurrection was accepted fully by his followers—none of which was inconsistent with Judaic thought, although many contested their views.

How ironic to denigrate the Jews. For Jesus (whose given name was Yeshua) died not as a Christian but the way he lived, as a Jew. He had never heard the word *Christianity;* he had no idea he would be called the founder of a separatist religion. His disciples were Jews: Saul, Shimon, and Levi were renamed Paul, Peter, and Matthew. Moreover, the early Christian Church was a Jewish sect firmly rooted in such Jewish precepts as the belief in the coming of a messiah and the idea of bodily resurrection.

Far from being "outsiders," Jews perceived Jesus as a descendant of a common lineage. Actually, Jews were the first to accept Jesus as their leader. Even though he may not have encouraged them, he symbolized for some their only hope of throwing off the oppressive weight of Roman tyranny.

Jews continued to look up to Jesus for decades until an all but impregnable wall was erected separating Gentile converts to Christianity from Jewish believers in Jesus.

Today an ever-growing number of Christians and Jews are committed to overcoming that barrier by questioning precepts handed down over the centuries concerning relationships between Jesus and Jews, Jews and Christians. Only then can we as citizens of "one nation under God" understand the teachings of Jesus, who warned that "every kingdom divided against itself is laid waste, and no city or house divided against itself will stand."

·4·

ONE GOD

What made it possible for Jesus to emerge from obscurity in Galilee to being revered by much of mankind?

His religion, Judaism, had developed a faith in a single omnipotent Supreme Being and the belief that man was made in God's image. These views acted as a civilizing force by encouraging mutual respect for all humanity. As no other nation or religious sect shared this concept, Jesus could not have emerged from any of the pagan religions, only from monotheistic Judaism.

The belief in one God was essential for the birth of Christianity since monotheism supports a universal moral code applicable to all, whereas in pagan cultures many gods represent a multiplicity of ethical standards. In fact, pagan gods were perceived to be in conflict with one another frequently, mirroring the dissonance of those who worshipped them. In Persia at that time, the gods Ormuzd and Ahriman were assumed to be in constant struggle.

Jesus could not have functioned in a polytheistic society, for he demanded total commitment to the covenantal relationship with God, a code of conduct, respect for fellow man and morality, which he derived from Jewish teachings. Conversely, members of a pagan culture could not be faithful to any one God.

Two thousand years before the birth of Jesus, the Hebrew Scriptures tells us that God revealed Himself in the hills of Hebron to an elderly nomad, Abram of Mesopotamia.

God established a covenant with Abram pledging that he would become the father of a community with a destiny and a promised land. Abram was so touched by God's revelation that he changed his name and the name of his wife, Sarai, to Abraham and Sarah. They became new people, united to God through this covenant and commission to testify to God in the world.

Now, after the passage of four thousand years, the concept of a single, all-powerful being may not appear an earthshaking departure. But considering the widespread worship of polytheistic deities and spirits, the superstitious rites and the custom of bloody human sacrifice practiced by neighboring nations, the acceptance of one God by the descendants of Abraham was the most sophisticated religious belief yet to be propounded.

Sun worship above all else prevailed over the many and varied Egyptian cults. When the soul of a dead pharaoh went to heaven it was to meet the sun, a privilege afforded to the ruling classes alone. This was contradictory to the one-God-for-all-people precept, without which Christianity could not have flourished.

Human sacrifice to earth gods and goddesses, especially at harvest time, was customary in ancient societies surrounding Palestine—Mesopotamia, Syria, and Egypt. In some of these rituals, ceremonies involved the spreading of blood from sacrificial victims on the earth at the beginning of the growing season to assure fertility. It would be difficult to envision a Jesus figure evolving out of such a culture.

In Babylonia, Anu was acclaimed "Sky King," father of the gods, and there were ten thousand lesser deities. Jupiter in Rome and Uranus and Zeus in Greece were believed to be cosmic divinities residing in the mountainous regions of the heavens where thunderbolts were released to strike down those who deserved punishment.

Though the tribes of Israel were surrounded by pagan worship, their tenacious acknowledgment of a single deity and their increasing insistence on preserving and cherishing human life developed, over many generations, into an all-encompassing religious commitment.

By the fourteenth century B.C.E., an alliance formed between certain migratory tribes that shaped Israel's future character. There were no images of God. He was ever present, but invisible. A movable ark (altar) accompanied nomadic Semites, whose dominant prayer was "Hear, O Israel, the Lord our God the Lord is One."

In the twelfth century B.C.E., northern and southern tribes were growing in number. Joshua, an Ephraimite, assembled twelve tribes at Shechem, a community in the central region of what is now Israel. The chieftains agreed to form a federation and swear that there would be only one God of Israel. Despite countless temptations and torment, for eight hundred years they and their followers had successfully withstood the pressures and seductions of their idolatrous neighbors.

For centuries, religious belief was handed down by word of mouth. No bodies of law had been written or assembled, there were no houses of worship or religious leaders. During the reign of King Josias (640–608 B.C.E.) an ancient book was discovered believed to represent the Deuteronomic law, probably compiled in the eighth century B.C.E. Assumed to be the writings of Moses, it was proclaimed the sacred law of Israel, and the city of Jerusalem was declared the geographic and religious center of Judaism.

But Israel was not to be left in peace. Babylonian armies attacked Jerusalem in 587 B.C.E. and deported the royal family and many skilled workmen. After the Babylonian exile Jews were allowed to return to Jerusalem to rebuild the city, the Temple, and the nation. They also started a movement that would change Judaism for centuries and deeply influence Jesus' vocation. It was the beginning of rabbinic Judaism, the Pharisaic movement that nurtured the spiritual development and learning of Jesus. Monotheism and the belief that God was ever present became, through the explanation and expansion of the biblical text, the very essence of Judaism, essential to the growth of Christianity.

This was affirmed by the Vatican Secretariat for Promoting Christian Unity in February 1970:

> In the Bible we observe that God reveals Himself concretely in events, in relations with real men: YHWH is the God of someone, of "Abraham of Isaac and of Jacob." God saves by acting. No fact or event eludes the design of "God the Saviour."
>
> Thus has the Jewish religion always conceived its relations with God.
>
> How then, in the Christian view, can we understand what "salvation history" means, that Revelation of God in and by history, without taking into consideration the manner in which the chosen people became aware of the encounter with God and lived this Revelation of a God ever present throughout its long history down to the present time?
>
> All believers, Jewish and Christian, have confronted the world of the "death of God," of *secularization*, or by whatever name one describes this placing of God in parentheses or excluding Him from His creation. . . . In face of this contemporary problem, the Jewish conception of the world as a permanent creation of God, of the living conception of the action and presence of the Creator in all His works—such a consensus can help us to remain faithful to the biblical sense of a sort of "consecration of the universe." . . .
>
> Jewish and Christian tradition, founded upon the word of God, is deeply conscious of the value of the human person, made in God's image. The love of the same God ought to be translated into efficacious action in

the interest of mankind. In the spirit of the prophets,
Jews and Christians will collaborate willingly in the
pursuit of social justice and peace. This cooperation
should extend to local, national, and international lev-
els. And joint action can also work toward a large measure of mutual knowledge and esteem.*

Within the structure of superstition, human sacrifice, and
polytheism, slavery was a universally cruel and accepted
custom in the ancient pagan world.

Jewish monotheists, conversely, sought to abolish the
deeply rooted slave system. They opposed enslavement of
one person by another and sought emancipation of slaves
with their families. Early legislation exposed the evils of
slavery, curbed the brutalities that prevailed in neighboring
lands, and ameliorated the hard lives of "hired servants"
(those who, because of ill fortune, had to sell themselves
into bondage).

Under religious law, the dignity of the laborer was safe-
guarded. He was not to be given any menial or degrading
work but only agricultural tasks or skilled labor such as
would be performed by a free laborer hired for a season.

*Introduction to the discussions of the plenary session of bishop members of
the Secretariat for Promoting Christian Unity, Rome, November 1969, quoted
from *Information Service* No. 9, February 1970/1, of the Secretariat for Promoting
Christian Unity.

·5·

JESUS AND JUDAISM

As the beneficiaries of an almost endless array of modern technological advances, it may be difficult for us to envision what life was like in Jesus' day. There were no miracle medicines to cure or ease the pain of almost certain death from leprosy, smallpox, tuberculosis, or myriad other diseases. There were no scientific explanations for the mysterious forces of nature—gravity, the tides, earthquakes, storms. Water was scarce and there were few sanitary facilities.

People existed for the most part in the foul grip of abject poverty. Police forces to protect the weak, societies to aid the poor, organizations to fight injustice—such institutions were unheard of. It was a time of overpowering superstition and turmoil.

Within this primitive framework, the Jews stood alone as ethical monotheists in a sea of pagan nations. Indeed, the most powerful of pagan empires, Rome, oppressed and ruled Palestine in those days through fear and intimidation. It was a time of overwhelming apprehension and unrest.

Internally, the Jewish community was administered by the Sadducees, a tiny religious establishment largely indifferent to the poverty of its people. The Pharisees, the Jewish sect Jesus related to, hoped to improve conditions by alleviating suffering. To some, Jesus was the answer to their prayers and to the prayers of countless generations of believers to follow.

· THE PREACHING OF JESUS ·

Initially, I was surprised at how easy it was for me as a Jew to relate to the teachings of Jesus. In retrospect, I see nothing unusual in this, for everything Jesus preached had its origins in Old Testament teachings, in particular the command to "love thy neighbor as thyself," which was singled out by the great Jewish scholar and sage Hillel (30 B.C.E.–9 C.E.) as the epitome of the Law.

This injunction from Leviticus 19:18 and other basic Jewish concepts from Genesis, Deuteronomy, Exodus, the Psalms, and the Prophets were incorporated by Jesus into his Sermon on the Mount:

> Blessed are the poor in spirit,
>   for theirs is the kingdom of heaven. . . .
> Blessed are the meek,
>   for they shall inherit the earth. . . .
> Blessed are the pure in heart,
>   for they shall see God.
> Blessed are the peacemakers,
>   for they shall be called sons of God.

Eight hundred years before the birth of Christ, the Hebrew prophets put forth such "Christian" concepts as "And what doth the Lord require of thee, but to do justly, and to love mercy and walk humbly with God." Jesus' great commandment of love in Matthew 22:37–40 is taken right out of God's instruction to Moses in Leviticus 19.

The understanding of the Jewishness of Jesus is reflected in the following passage from a document issued by the Vatican Secretariat for Promoting Christian Unity: "Jesus,

as also His disciples, was a Jew. He presented Himself as
continuing and fulfilling the anterior Revelation, the basic
teachings of which He offered anew, using the same teaching method as the rabbis of His time. The points on which
He took issue with the Judaism of His time are fewer than
those in which He found Himself in agreement with it.
Whenever He opposed it, this was always from within the
Jewish people, just as did the prophets before Him.''*

Christianity embraces the beliefs embodied in the Hebrew Scriptures. The concepts of hell, heaven, angels, and
devils; the acceptance of Adam and Eve as the first man
and woman; the creation of the world in seven days; and
even its age, four thousand years—all are basic Hebrew
beliefs accepted even today by strict fundamentalists.

Jewish influences are also apparent in the structure of
church services, which are patterned on synagogue customs,
with the Hebrew Psalms playing a crucial role in both Catholic and Protestant prayers; in the Eucharist or Mass, which
incorporates such traditional Jewish Passover customs as
the breaking of bread and the "use of the cup"; and in the
adaptation of the words *amen* and *hallelujah*, the Lord's
Prayer, and the ritual of baptism. Until the end of the third
century, Christians in many provinces celebrated Easter on
Passover.

Just as surprising is the extent to which Jesus conformed
to rabbinical standards of his day, for it was customary for
teachers then to spend a great deal of time among the poor
in attempts to treat those who were ill, provide food for
those who were destitute, and perform other concrete acts
of mercy. These were specific requirements of Pharisaic
tradition.

The observance of the Sabbath was crucial in Hebrew
teaching as a reminder of the goodness of creation and a

Information Service No. 9, February 1970/1, of the Secretariat for Promoting
Christian Unity.

sign of the covenantal relationship between God and His chosen people.

Any sort of work on the Sabbath was frowned on as a violation of established ritual, as is pointed out in Exodus 34:21: "Six days thou shalt work, but on the seventh day, thou shalt rest; in earing (grain) time and in harvest thou shalt rest."

Certain Pharisaic followers carried this observance to an extreme by insisting, for example, that healers could not aid the sick on the Sabbath. Jesus' desire to ameliorate such conditions had its origins within Judaism, particularly in a group of learned men led by Hillel, who, before the birth of Jesus, had been interpreting the Law of Moses in conformity with the needs of the spirit and the demands of everyday life. Like Jesus, these early reformers believed that inner motivation determines righteousness as much as external form or ritual, and that the Sabbath was meant for man and not man for the Sabbath (Mark 2:27).

While others emphasized brotherly love, Jesus carried the ideals of Hillel to the ultimate by advocating loving one's enemies. Building on this, he elevated an original Jewish concept to a primary precept of Christianity.

Significantly, Jesus was a product of a tradition of disputation within Judaism. Just as there are divergent elements within Christianity and Judaism today, so were there diverse sects within Judaism in Jesus' day. Under such conditions Jesus did not hesitate to rail against empty religious strictures and to express displeasure over certain practices of some sects. However, one should not conclude from this that Jesus was anti-Jewish, any more than Luther or Calvin were anti-Christian from their criticism of Catholicism.

Jesus was adamant on this subject when he said: "And when you pray, you must not be like the hypocrites [a word used by the Pharisees]; for they love to stand and pray in the synagogues and at the street corners, that they may be seen by men. Truly, I say to you, they have received their reward. But when you pray, go into your room and shut the door and pray to your Father who is in secret; and your Father who sees in secret will reward you. And in praying do not heap empty phrases as the Gentiles do; for they think that they will be heard for their many words. Do not be like them, for your Father knows what you need before you ask him" (Matthew 6:5–8).

I feel close to Jesus because the values of Judaism are apparent in everything he taught and did. Every aspect of his life, including the Last Supper, a ritual of the Passover celebration was in that tradition. I have even come to believe, in the light of the Nazi Holocaust, that Jesus' last words on the cross, which are the opening words of Psalm 22, are central to my experience as a Jew: "My God, my God, why hast thou forsaken me? Why art thou so far from helping me, from the words of my groaning?"

Anyone who wants to relate to Jesus must understand his life as a Jew. As Bishop John Shelby Spong wrote in *This Hebrew Lord*, "I am convinced that if the Bible is going to be understood in our day we must develop 'Hebrew eyes' and 'Hebrew attitudes' toward life. The Bible is a Hebrew book, telling the story of the Hebrew people. Jesus was a Hebrew Lord."

• WHO WERE THE FOLLOWERS OF JESUS? •

Jesus' first followers—the *am ha-aretz*, the poor and unlearned, whom he encountered on the roads and hillsides of his native Galilee—were exclusively Jewish. Moreover, Jesus' earliest disciples were Jews faithful to the laws and traditions of Israel. According to Acts 1:13, they were "Peter and John and James and Andrew, Philip and Thomas, Bartholomew and Matthew, James the son of Alphaeus and Simon the Zealot and Judas the son of James." Judas Iscariot by now is omitted from this listing of the Twelve, and Paul only took up his mission sometime later.

Long after Jesus' death, as "pillars of the church," they continued to observe the commandments of Moses, to worship in the Temple, and to circumcise their children in accordance with Jesus' declaration in Matthew 5:18 that "till heaven and earth pass away, not an iota, not a dot, will pass from [Judaic] law until all is accomplished."

So imbued were Jesus' disciples with the traditions of Judaism in those early days that they and their fellow believers were Jews not only in their own eyes, but also in the eyes of the religious establishment. Otherwise they would not have been allowed to pray in the Temple, the central edifice of Jewish worship.

For years these and subsequent followers of Christ practiced their faith in synagogues. "The Synagogue looked upon the movement as just another sect," writes Father Edward H. Flannery in *The Anguish of the Jews*. "The early Christian church, full of zeal and fervor, was a Jewish church in leadership, membership and worship; and it remained within the precincts of the Synagogue."

• THE COMING OF THE MESSIAH •

For generations the word had been passed down among Jews that through the intervention of the Messiah, which in Hebrew means the anointed one or king, God would redeem Israel from oppression. So fundamental is this belief to the Jewish experience that it has been called the most glistening jewel in the glorious crown of Judaism.

The Messiah was expected in Jesus' day to destroy the power of Rome over Palestine, to replace the existing king with a descendant of David, and to spur and enable Jews throughout the world to return from exile to their homeland. It was widely believed that events of such magnitude would bring about the long-awaited final judgment of God, followed by another important Jewish belief, the resurrection of the dead. "Thy dead shall live, my body shall arise" (Isaiah 26:19). "I believe with perfect faith that there will be a revival of the dead at the time when it please the creator" (Maimonides, *Commentary on the Mishnah*, Sanhedrin 1168, 10, 1. Thirteen Principles, no. 13).

The quotation from Isaiah, eight centuries before the birth of Jesus, and from Maimonides, twelve centuries after his birth, illustrate the tenacity of this belief among Jews.

As long as he preached, Jesus attracted large numbers of Jewish followers who believed him to be their messiah. It was, in fact, his potential unification of a wide group of followers, which posed a threat to Roman rule, that led to Christ's trial and conviction. For many Jews it was only after his death that their belief in Jesus as their messiah was shaken, for Judaism had no tradition of a dying messiah, only of one who would continue to lead them and bring relief from the burdens imposed on them by Roman tyranny.

·6·

THE CRUCIFIXION

Christian anti-Semitism as I know it today did not exist in the time of Jesus, for no major distinction had yet been made between the Jewish followers of Jesus and other Jews. With the emergence of the Gospels, more than three decades after the death of Jesus, major differences arose between these two groups, resulting in the birth of Christian anti-Semitism.

The Gospels reflected neither Jesus' compassion for his fellow Jews, nor his reverence for the religion he had practiced all his life. It was the desire of some early leaders to take the new sect out of the synagogue and create a separate and distinct religion. The intention was to free Christianity from the womb of Judaism in order to more easily indoctrinate and effect conversions.

This may partially explain the puzzling hostility to the Jews expressed in the Gospels, which diminished the Jewishness of Jesus, emphasized differences between Christianity and Judaism, and stigmatized the Jews. One of the great mysteries of past ages is the inclusion of anti-Semitic passages in the Gospels since three of the four narrators—Mark, Matthew, and John—were themselves Jewish, became Jewish Christians, and venerated the Jewish Jesus. It is unthinkable that they would deliberately condemn their coreligionists to centuries of degradation. Matthew, whose

32

name was Levi, was a tax collector. John, whose Jewish name was Yohanan, was a fisherman in the Sea of Galilee.

While the Gospels were formulated between 70 C.E. and 100 C.E., no manuscripts of the Gospels prior to the fourth century actually exist today. It would seem possible that, as the Christian faith developed and as the number of Jewish Christians declined during the three hundred years after the death of Jesus, revisions exceedingly critical of the Jews were added to original texts.

It is conceivable in particular that segments of the New Testament dealing with the part Jews were alleged to have played in the crucifixion could have been modified. We are told, for example, that the Jews clamored for the death of Jesus. Which Jews? Were they his Jewish disciples and the crowd that accompanied him to Jerusalem at Passover? Or were they, in fact, a few panic-stricken members of the Sanhedrin, beholden to Roman occupiers and fearful of bloody reprisals against the whole Jewish people, who without approval of other council members summoned Jesus in the dead of night, disregarding all established Jewish judicial policy. Placing the blame for the crucifixion of Jesus on all "the Jews" unjustly has led to devastating repercussions down through the centuries.

Reshaping events already veiled by the passage of time is confirmed by eminent historians, including Father John A. Hardon in *Christianity in the Twentieth Century*, who concedes that the "dynamism which produced the Gospels was not a desire to preserve the memory of what Jesus had preached, but a need to serve a nascent community that was mysteriously inspired to worship and follow a great leader." What developed, according to Father Hardon, was a tendency to "obscure and embellish, if not distort, the facts to meet the demands of an idealistic faith," so that religious instruction, constantly repeated, conditioning successive generations with mythical arguments, became part of history. After hundreds of years myths take on the semblance of reality and are perceived as events that happened exactly as portrayed.

The most tragic result, according to Protestant scholar Bernhard E. Olsen, in *Faith and Prejudice,* is that "in most Christian churches children are taught that the Jews killed Jesus [even though] many Christians have come to the conclusion that it was the Romans who killed Jesus, not the Jews. But many churches continue to teach the old story just the same. The result is that countless Christian children begin life with a prejudice: the Jews who killed Jesus (two thousand years ago), as they are told, are the same to them as the Jews who live on the next block."

In order to counteract such attitudes, I would like to review the principal events that led to Jesus' death in the light of what we know about political and religious conditions in his day.

The most salient fact is that Israel, as a vassal state of Rome, had no power to try anyone on political grounds. It was only within the power of the central authority of Israel (the Sanhedrin) to punish Jews for religious infractions. The Sanhedrin had little fault to find with Jesus within their area of responsibility since he did not violate any of the major precepts of their mutual faith.

Malachi Martin, in his monumental book *The Encounter,* comes to the same conclusion:

> Jesus was not tried and condemned either because he assured men that their sins were forgiven by him or anyone else, or for supposedly making light of certain Levitical laws of purity, or for healing on the Sabbath, or for driving devils out of the possessed in the name of Beelzebub, or for his attitude to fasting, or for plotting the destruction of the Temple, or for claiming to be the Messiah, or for blaspheming by saying that he was the Son of Man, or because the Pharisees were loyal

to the Romans, or because the Sadducees were corrupt, or because the Jewish people as a whole clamored for his death, or because the Pharisees and Sadducees were jealous of his power and popularity, or because Jesus proposed to abrogate the Law of Moses.

What alarmed the Sanhedrin had little if anything to do with such matters. Rather, as word spread of the miracles Jesus performed and his fame increased, it would appear that Jesus began to alarm the priestly establishment as a *political* force. Lauded as a messiah, he was regarded by his followers as someone who could free Israel from Roman oppression.

The Gospels tells us that the Jewish high priest Caiaphas turned Jesus over to Pontius Pilate. Actually, Caiaphas was a Roman collaborator. In his book *Faith without Prejudice*, Eugene Fisher, of the National Conference of Catholic Bishops, confirms that "The chief priest was appointed by Rome and held office at the will of Rome. The Roman procurator even kept the chief priest's vestments. If the Roman authorities became displeased with a high priest, he was deposed and a new one, more suitable to Rome, was appointed. In this sense, the chief priest cannot fairly be called a 'Jewish' leader at all. Though always a Jew by birth, he gave loyalty only to Rome and did the will of Rome."

It must be borne in mind that the situation at that time was so precarious that the survival of the entire Jewish nation was at stake. Many Jews had already been crucified by the Romans and any provocation could kindle a revolt, which would almost certainly lead to even more oppression. Caiaphas apparently had no alternative but to turn over one man to the Romans at once in order to avoid endangering an entire population.

Shortly thereafter, the Jewish historian Josephus reports that a Roman guarding the courtyard of the Temple during

Passover ridiculed the worshippers, thus causing a riot in which thirty thousand people lost their lives. In the light of such volatile conditions, the council's concern over the consequences of Jesus' activities can be better appreciated.

Even John, the most persistent denigrator of Jews in the New Testament, must have recognized the political necessity of the council's reasoning. For he lived to see a monumental uprising against Rome take place some years after Jesus' death, an uprising that ended in the destruction of the Temple, the devastation of Jerusalem, and the decimation of its population.

If under such circumstances certain priests felt they had to turn Jesus over to the Romans, this in no way alters the fact that Jesus was executed, as Malachi Martin puts it, "after a Roman indictment before a Roman official who imposed a Roman capital punishment for a crime against Rome and who entrusted the performance of this legal sentence to Roman subordinate officials and soldiers."

The Roman historian Tacitus, in his voluminous annals drawn from official Roman public records, wrote, "Christus, from whom the name [Christian] had its origin, suffered the extreme penalty during the reign of Tiberius at the hands of one of our procurators [governors], Pontius Pilate."

Prior to Pilate's appointment, Roman procurators had ruled Palestine in relative peace. Immediately upon his appointment, Pilate moved Roman headquarters from Caesarea to Jerusalem, thus aggravating an already explosive situation. His troops stationed there were a constant provocation to the Jews, especially at Passover, when the Roman presence was particularly resented.

Pilate is described in the Gospels as a fainthearted weakling who merely acquiesced to the demands of "the Jews." Nothing could be farther from the truth. He is described by historians of the time as a man of inflexible disposition whose insolence, rapacity, and hunger for cruelty led him in numerous cases to order the crucifixion of people without trial.

Jesus was executed in customary Roman fashion. A century before Jesus' death, a slave named Spartacus led an insurrection that was eventually suppressed by praetor Marcus Licinius Crassus. In accordance with official Roman policy, Crassus crucified six thousand of the rebellious slaves on crosses lining the road from Rome to Capua to serve as a warning to others who might have similar ideas. Crucifixion continued to be the standard form of legal punishment until the fourth century C.E.

Despite the overriding evidence of their innocence, "the Jews" have been stigmatized and held accountable for acts that occurred one hundred generations ago. Is it only for Jews that time and reason are suspended in so bizarre a fashion? Is a little boy in the twentieth century a Christ killer? Were children murdered by the Nazis in any way connected to the purported complicity of a handful of individuals almost two thousand years ago?

By the same token, are all Christians accountable for the death of President John F. Kennedy? Are all Moslems responsible for the assassination of Robert Kennedy? All Catholics for the burning of Protestants during the Spanish Inquisition? All Germans for the crimes of the Nazis? Are you yourself answerable for the deeds of your grandfather?

Would Jesus have tolerated such actions against his father, his teachers, his friends and acquaintances, all of whom were practicing Jews? Surely he would have been appalled by the strange twist of unforeseen events that isolated him from the people he loved. Yet every Jew, from Jesus' contemporaries to those of every generation to the end of time, is declared guilty of his death by the very people who found salvation in his suffering.

·7·

CHRISTIANITY AND ANTI-SEMITISM

Why did Judaism have to be degraded in order to validate Christianity? Christianity as a sect of Judaism was bogged down on several issues, of which circumcision was perhaps the most perplexing.

Jewish members of the Christian sect were "painlessly" circumcised on the eighth day of life. Non-Jewish members of the sect, however, had to become Jews in order to be saved, and thus had to undergo the pain and danger of adult circumcision.

Pagans did not relish taking up a religion that would entail great suffering and anguish. Realizing the improbability of attracting a sufficient number of supplicants if circumcision was a precondition, the leaders of the sect decided that adult circumcision would have to be abolished in order for Christianity to grow in numbers and strength.

A council of Nazarenes was convened in Jerusalem in about 50 C.E. and attended by the Jewish followers of Jesus and a number of influential converts. With the prompting of Paul and Peter, it was agreed that spiritual sons of Abraham could not by mere circumcision become physical sons of Abraham. Under their leadership it was generally agreed to accept pagans into the new sect while maintaining its

Jewishness, but releasing converts from the painful necessity of undergoing circumcision.

A letter was formulated and dispatched to Antioch in which it was stated that henceforth non-Jews need not be circumcised in order to become Christians. The letter began:

> The Apostles and Elders who are your brothers send their greetings to the brothers who are Gentiles in Antioch, Syria and Cicilia. Since we have heard that some of our number have caused you deep distress [by insisting on circumcision] and have unsettled your minds by giving you a message which certainly did not originate with us, we are unanimously agreed to send you chosen representatives . . . who will give you the same message personally by word of mouth. For it has seemed right to the Holy Spirit and to us to lay no further burden upon you except what is absolutely essential, namely, that you avoid what has been sacrificed to idols, testing blood, eating the meat of what has been strangled, and sexual immorality. Keep yourselves clear of these things and you will make good progress. Farewell. (Acts 15:23–29)

The council of Jerusalem, the first of its kind, represented a turning point in history; the eventual consequences of that meeting could be considered the beginning of Christianity. Despite the appearance of a seemingly conciliatory agreement, its participants were divided into two angry camps.

One faction believed that converts to Jewish Christianity should be circumcised and should conform to all Judaic laws. The other faction, led by Paul of Tarsus, strongly contradicted this viewpoint, claiming that circumcision and adherence to Mosaic law were unnecessary burdens for Gentile converts.

Paul, whose original name was Saul, was Jewish by birth. He proudly describes himself in the Letter to the Philippians as "circumcised on the eighth day, of the people of Israel, of the tribe of Benjamin, a Hebrew born of Hebrews" (3:5).

Although he had never known Jesus, he became an early and staunch supporter, repudiated Judaism despite his ambivalent feelings in order to proselytize pagans to accept Christianity. In the end, what appeared to be a minor compromise in the letter to Antioch and other Gentile communities resulted in a major victory for Paul.

This message had an enormous impact on the future of Christianity. "As they [the chosen representatives, Paul and Timothy] went on their way through the cities, they passed on to them [potential converts] for their observance the decisions which had been reached by the Apostles and Elders in Jerusalem. Consequently, the Churches grew stronger and stronger in the faith and their numbers increased daily" (Acts 16:4).

Paul asserts that on his way to Damascus (Acts 9:3) he saw a great light from heaven and Jesus spoke to him as the Lord. Thus Christianity began to distance itself further from Judaism since Jews, while believing in the coming of a Messiah, could not accept the divinity of any human being, even Abraham or Moses. In fact, Maimonides, the great twelfth-century Jewish scholar, makes it an article of Jewish faith that "God has no bodily image nor human form."

At this moment in history, most Jews live outside Palestine. They were dispersed throughout the lands and possessions of the Roman Empire and their monotheism had gained a measure of respect. We cannot minimize the fact that the spread of Christianity was made easier for proselytizers wherever Jews had already settled, for these Jews, by practicing many of the customs carried over into Christianity, made the new faith all the more accessible to the pagan mind.

Nevertheless, early Christians realized that in order for

their movement to expand they would have to make it even more attractive to non-Jews. This they did by freeing their movement from all Jewish laws and customs that served to reinforce Judaism's commitment to exclusivity.

There was a reason for final alienation. Judaism, in a state of disarray, appeared to be a dying religion. In 66 C.E., Roman governor Gessius Florus had crucified three thousand Jews for provoking a revolt that had ended in the destruction of the Temple and the razing of Jersusalem. (The Jewish/Christian synagogue had been removed to Antioch just prior to this debacle.) The Jews no longer existed as a state. Judaism could be attacked and condemned, and future generations, if there were any, could be damned with little worry of repercussions.·

But Christians had a great deal to fear from Rome. As early as 64 C.E. they were being persecuted by Nero. They were nonetheless dependent on Rome as the center of their growing movement, and as a small sect they could not risk offending the governing powers. It was imperative to exonerate Caesar's representatives for Jesus' death. The Gospels attempted to accomplish this by portraying Pilate as an incompetent who merely carried out the wishes of "the Jews." (In reality, he neither wanted nor required Jewish consent to crucify Jesus.)

The four Gospels were formulated within thirty years after the fall of the Temple. All of the Gospels reflect the political expediency of blaming "the Jews" for Jesus' death even though Jesus himself expressed love for his Jewish brethren.

But Christians failed to mollify the Romans, their avowed enemies. For nearly three hundred years, Rome continued to persecute Christians. It was not until the Emperor Constantine entered into an alliance with Christianity early in the fourth century that Roman persecution came to an end.

·8·

ROME AND EARLY CHRISTIANITY

From its stormy birth in Palestine, Christianity grav- itated toward Rome, by this time the center of the civilized world. Eugene J. Fisher, of the National Confer- ence of Catholic Bishops, observes that the Gospels were written at this time when the very survival of the Church depended on Roman tolerance: "It was not expedient to condemn Rome when Christianity was [beginning to be] successful in converting Romans." The Jews, now widely dispersed, no longer a nation, were easier, more vulnerable targets.

But the new sect was not welcomed by an establishment that was uncertain of its own destiny. Christians were used as scapegoats at the whim of any emperor in power, espe- cially when they served as convenient justification for the continuing economic, political, and military decline of the empire.

Tacitus reveals that Nero, as a tactic to divert attention from his own guilt in starting fires, "substituted as culprits and punished with the utmost cruelty, a class of persons hated for their vices, whom the crowd called Christians. Christus, the founder of the name, had undergone the death penalty in the region of Tiberius, by sentence of the procurator Pontius Pilate, and the pernicious superstition was checked for a moment, only to break out once more, not only in Judea, the home of the disease, but in the capital itself, where everything horrible or shameful in the world gathers and becomes fashionable."

Persecution merely strengthened Christian opposition to worshipping the Roman gods Jupiter, Jove, Juno, Eros, Diana, Hera, Apollo, Saturn, or any other pagan divinity. Christians refused to participate in sun worship, Mithraism, which originated in Persia, and what was most galling to Romans was Christian rejection of the emperor as a deity.

The holiday for Saturn, Roman god of agriculture, was particularly difficult to resist. It was a week-long celebration terminating on December 25. There was much partying, gift giving, and conviviality; all business was put aside; and slaves were released temporarily from their work. The debauchery that occurred during the Saturnalia did not sit well with the Christians. In retaliation for their lack of participation, they were charged with constituting a felonious covert society that drank blood and ate human flesh as a part of their religious rituals.

Suetonius, official historian of the Roman court, scorned Christianity, saying "punishment was justly inflicted on the Christians, a class of persons given to a new and maleficent superstition." Tacitus believed in solving the "Christian problem" permanently, describing a typical incident: "First then those of the [Christian] sect were arrested who confessed; next on their disclosures, vast numbers were convicted, not so much on the count of arson as for hatred of the human race. And ridicule accompanied their end: they were covered with wild beast skins and torn to death by dogs; or they were fastened on crosses and when daylight failed, were burned to serve as torches by night. Nero offered his garden for the spectacle."

It finally became mandatory for any Roman judge or administrator to investigate a person suspected of being a

Christian. The Emperor Trajan, who reigned from 98–117 C.E., received the following letter from Pliny the Younger, Roman governor of the provinces of Bithynia and Pontica:

> It is my custom, Lord Emperor, to refer to you all questions whereof I am in doubt. Who can better guide me? . . . I have never participated in investigation of Christians; hence I do not know what is the crime usually punished or investigated, or what allowances are made. . . . Meanwhile, this is the course I have taken with those who were accused before me as Christians. I asked them whether they were Christians, and I asked them a second and third time with threats of punishment. If they kept to it, I ordered them taken off for execution, for I had no doubt that whatever it was they admitted, in any case they deserve to be punished for obstinacy and unbending pertinacity. . . . As for those who said they neither were nor ever had been Christians, I thought it right to let them go, when they recited a prayer to the gods at my dictation, and made supplication with incense and wine to your statue, which I had ordered to be brought into court for the purpose, and moreover, cursed Christ—things which (so it was said) those who are really Christians cannot be made to do.

The Emperor Trajan was a soldier who had decisively defeated the powerful Parthians. As a military man, he had no patience with a people who, along with other "faults," disapproved of army service.

Trajan's approval of Pliny's actions was immediate:

> You have adopted the proper course, my dear Secundus, in your examination of the cases of those who were accused before you as Christians, for indeed, nothing can be laid down as a general rule involving something like a set form of procedure. They are not to be sought

out; but if they are accused and convicted, they must be punished—but on the condition that whoever denies that he is a Christian, and makes the fact plain by his action, that is, by worshipping our gods, shall obtain pardon on his repentance, however suspicious his past conduct may be.

Some idea of the pagan Roman character can be gleaned from practices accepted as normal. Debtors were not only imprisoned, but were also scourged and their faces branded. Kidnapping of children was a common crime that usually went unpunished. Children could be sold at birth. A slave could be crucified at the whim of his master. Horses and field animals were beaten until they dropped. This, then, was the atmosphere of ancient Rome.

This brief recounting of the cruelties inflicted on a courageous people and their ultimate triumph over evil gives only a partial picture of a terrible historical process whereby today's victims become tomorrow's victimizers.

Christians who were accused by the Romans of drinking human blood in their religious rituals used the same accusation against the Jews. A *permanent solution* was sought by the Romans for the "Christian problem." Substitute "Jewish problem" and bigotry can be updated to the twentieth century. It was mandatory for a Roman judge to conduct an inquisition against any person accused of being a Christian. Identical instructions later plagued those of the Jewish faith. Christianity endured a nightmare of Roman excesses: scourging, burning, and crucifixion. Later, Jews were tortured by Christians in similar if not identical ways.

Christianity replaced paganism, but for Jews many of the persecutions that were pagan in origin have persisted for two thousand years.

Within a hundred years after Jesus' death Jewish Christians who believed in him had all but disappeared, and by 200 C.E. ties with Jerusalem ceased to exist.

By then, non-Roman emperors were in control of the empire and they were contemptuous of most of its former traditions. As the state became irresolute and impotent, Christianity became more robust and self-sufficient.

In 313 C.E., an event of enormous importance to Christianity occurred. Emperor Constantine issued an "edict of toleration, freedom of worship and the return of confiscated property." After surviving a Roman cauldron of hate and prejudice, Christianity had reached a turning point; the fourth century marked the beginning of its temporal power and the eventual domination of the empire and all its territories.

·9·

BOOMERANG

"**T**errible things have been done in Jesus' name; the doctrine of unworldliness which he preached has been twisted to serve worldly purposes. The cross on which he died, besides inspiring some of the noblest lives which have ever been lived, and some of the noblest thoughts and creations of man, has also been enforced with the rack and the whip, and driven home with the sword."*

A Christian might well wonder how the above statement applies to him or her. Actually, it involves all of us; doctrines based on hostility to any one group inevitably encompass all groups.

The tragic consequences of the Spanish Inquisition are a case in point. In the beginning the Catholic Church persecuted Jews for worshipping a "foreign god." But soon officials of the Inquisition also began to torture and burn Protestants for refusing to adhere to the strictures of Catholic Orthodoxy.

Eventually, Catholics themselves were jeopardized; thousands imprisoned and put to death as heretics. Ultimately, no one was above suspicion. In a single day, an honorable Catholic family of "pure blood" could be stripped of all its

---

*Malcolm Muggeridge, *Jesus Rediscovered* (Garden City, NY: Doubleday, 1979).

possessions merely because of some fancied slight to an official of the all-powerful Inquisition.

As for Spain, by the mid-1600s its glory was only a memory. Its once-powerful fleet was by now disbanded, its people in ferment, its economic structure in ruins. Spain was no longer among the most powerful nations in the world—largely because a credo of hate destroyed its unity, contributing to its decline.

* * * * *

In 1884, a French army officer's espionage for Germany started a chain of events that shook the French republic, exposed the General Staff as liars, and divided the nation for years.

Born in Paris of Hungarian descent, Major Marie Charles Ferdinand Walsin Esterhazy was a scoundrel who had dissipated his aristocratic wife's fortune. He was heavily in debt and was notorious for his shady financial dealings. In July 1884, Esterhazy visited the German embassy in Paris and offered his services as a spy to the German military attaché, Colonel Max von Schwartzkoppen.

Sometime after that, a French colonel visiting the German embassy noticed a batch of incoming mail destined for von Schwartzkoppen. Realizing that someone in a responsible position was revealing military plans, he surreptitiously seized a document handwritten in French that had been placed there only moments before by Esterhazy. It was signed "D." Later, poring through a list of officers, the General Staff investigators came to the name Dreyfus. Disregarding the obvious—no traitor would conceivably use his own initial—they nonetheless came to an immediate wish-fulfilling conclusion: "It was the Jew!"

The Jew was Captain Alfred Dreyfus, an Alsatian, "more French than the French." Quiet, reserved, loyal, the army had been his entire career.

Although the indictment against him was spurious, Dreyfus was pronounced guilty by a military court. Before his sentencing, he was offered a garden spot (instead of Devil's Island), with his family to accompany him, if he would confess, not to treason, but to a moment of carelessness. Dreyfus refused, asking only that the actual traitor be found so that his name could be cleared.

Captain Dreyfus was humiliated in a public ceremony, his sword broken, his epaulets stripped from his uniform. The crowd roared, "Death to the Jew!" Imprisoned in a stone hut on Devil's Island surrounded by a wall eight feet high, Dreyfus was completely isolated. Later a second wall, even higher, was constructed so that he could see nothing. When he slept, iron bands were locked around his ankles, and he was forbidden to exchange a word with his guards.

Some eighteen months after the trial, General de Boisdeffre, curious as to what would induce a brilliant officer to betray his country, requested an intelligence officer, Colonel Picquart, to review the Dreyfus file.

Picquart examined the evidence and to his astonishment noted that the *single* piece of incriminating evidence was not in Dreyfus' handwriting. Boisdeffre suggested that the document be shown to General Gonse. The general raged, "The Dreyfus case is closed." Meanwhile, Esterhazy had been exposed, but no action was taken against him. To the General Staff, establishing the guilt of Esterhazy would only prove the innocence of Dreyfus.

The French newspapers continued to stir up controversy against a "Jewish syndicate"; there were orgies of hate and anti-Semitism while Dreyfus deteriorated on Devil's Island. "Kill the Jews," "No vote for Jews," "Expel the Jews," cried the mobs.

When Esterhazy was finally brought to court, he was acquitted, but Picquart was arrested. The rest of the world grieved for a France where justice no longer prevailed. Sob-

bing as he read the foreign newspapers, French statesman
Georges Clemenceau wrote:

> France discovered certain human rights of justice and
> liberty . . . mirrored in the beautiful words: Every man
> has two countries, his own and France. For a country
> is [valued] not only for its soil, forests and fields . . . but
> also for the ideas that knit souls together, the actions
> of the people, their influence on the civilized world.
> When it will be perceived that right and justice in our
> country are words deprived of significance, that brute
> force has become the only arbiter, when once more we
> shall have become persecutors of races and reli-
> gions . . . when the watchwords of tolerance and liberty
> will have yielded to the clamors of hatred then, we
> may still have the same fields, the same rivers, the
> same mountains. We may still sit on French soil. But
> we shall have ceased to be the France our fathers de-
> sired to create.

Civiltà Cattolica, the official newspaper of the Jesuit order
of Rome, joined the fray: "The Jew was created by God to
serve as a spy wherever treason is in preparation . . . anti-
Semitism will become, as it should, economic, political,
national . . . not only in France, but in Germany, Austria
and Italy, Jews are to be excluded from the nation. Then
the old harmony will be reestablished and the peoples will
again find all their lost happiness." The Vatican agreed,
saying, "The duty of every good Catholic is to stand behind
Premier Meline in his anti-Semitic endeavors."

A storm arose in Catholic communities everywhere—in
Ireland, the European continent, the United States, and South
America—condemning these attitudes. In France itself,
hundreds of Catholics set up a committee dedicated to "the
defense of right and justice." The prince of Monaco, a devout

Catholic, journeyed to Germany to inquire of the emperor whether Dreyfus had been involved in espionage. The emperor confirmed that it was not Dreyfus, but Esterhazy who was the spy. The prince of Monaco then appealed to the president of France, to no avail.

Out of this discord, a new note was sounded, inevitable in a bigoted cover-up of this magnitude—the Protestants and Masons were charged, along with the Jews, of undermining France.

On January 13, 1898, with France in turmoil, an open letter addressed to Felix Faure, president of the republic, appeared in the newspaper *L'Aurore.* Under the heading *J'Accuse,* French novelist Emile Zola's words had the force of a tornado:

> A court-martial has . . . dared to acquit one Esterhazy—a supreme slap at all truth, all justice: And it is done. France has this brand upon her image; history will relate that it was during your administration that such a social crime could be committed.
>
> My duty is to speak. My nights would be haunted by the specter of the innocent being [incarcerated] under the most frightful torture, a crime he never committed.
>
> The truth, first, on the trial and condemnation of Dreyfus. One pernicious individual arranged, planned, concocted everything—Colonel du Paty de Clam. He is the whole Dreyfus affair . . . the one who is most guilty of the fearful miscarriage of justice.
>
> I accuse Colonel du Paty de Clam of having been the diabolical agent of the judicial error and of having continued to defend his deadly work during the past three years through the most absurd and revolting machinations.
>
> I accuse General Mercier of having made himself an accomplice in one of the greatest crimes in history.
>
> I accuse General Billot of having had in his hands

the decisive proof of the innocence of Dreyfus and of having concealed it and of having rendered himself guilty of the crime of lese humanity and lese justice, out of political motives and to save the face of the General Staff.

I accuse General Pellieux and Major Ravary of having held a scoundrelly inquest of the most monstrous partiality, the complete report of which composes for us an imperishable monument of naive effrontery.

I accuse the three handwriting experts, MM. Belhomme, Varinard and Couard, of having made lying and fraudulent reports, unless a medical examination will certify them to be deficient of sight and judgment.

I accuse the War Office of having led a vile campaign in the press, particularly in the *Echo de Paris* and in *L'Eclair*, in order to misdirect public opinion and cover up its sins.

I accuse, lastly, the first court-martial of having violated all human rights in condemning a prisoner on testimony kept secret from him, and I accuse the second court-martial of having covered up this illegality by order, committing in turn the judicial crime of acquitting a guilty man with full knowledge of his guilt.

The action I take here is simply a revolutionary step designed to hasten the explosion of truth and justice.

I have one passion only, for light, in the name of humanity which has borne so much and has a right to happiness. My burning protest is only the cry of my soul. Let them dare to carry me to the court of appeals, and let there be an inquest in the full light of day!

I am waiting.

From every part of the world, letters by the tens of thousands poured into France applauding Zola's protest. In America, Mark Twain proclaimed, "I am penetrated with the most profound respect for Zola. Such cowards, hypocrites as the members of military and ecclesiastic courts the world could produce by the million every year. But it takes five centuries to produce a Joan of Arc or a Zola."

Unfortunately, the rabble-rousers and bigots were in control. Zola was tried for criminal libel and convicted in a courtroom packed with hoodlums. He fled to England rather than serve a jail sentence. Zola died in 1902. In his funeral oration, Anatole France said, "Do not pity him for what he had to endure and suffer. Envy him! He had deserved well of the country, as he had of the world by an immense life-work and a great act. Fate and his courage swept him to the summit; to be, for one instant, the conscience of mankind."

The decline of justice in France was mourned by leaders in England, Sweden, Belgium, and the Netherlands. Even czarist Russian newspapers asked, "Does France still have the right to be called the nation of enlightenment?"

But mass hysteria still convulsed France. Zola was hung in effigy. Mobs attacked Jews and broke into shops in France and French-controlled Algeria, where Arabs, for once, gleefully joined with the French in vicious pogroms.

In his extraordinary book *Captain Dreyfus*, Nicholas Halasz writes, "The country was possessed of violent excitement. No time, thought or passion seemed left for the business of everyday life. Life consisted of turning to the papers, arming oneself with arguments, fighting with the word and the fist. People ceased to read books or to go to the theatre. No thriller, no play could compete with the drama of which France was the stage, her citizens the actors, and the civilized world the audience. This fever was destined to keep a hold of varying intensity on the country for years."

Bigotry is costly: About this time, France was further disgraced by an international incident in Africa. A small team had found its way to the upper Nile and had raised the French flag. Control of the Nile at its source would have assured dominance over Egypt and the Sudan, but the British under Lord Kitchener threatened to attack France's seaports unless they withdrew. Incapable of action, the French government retreated.

The injustice done to Dreyfus finally ended. On July 12, 1906, the French high court declared him innocent of all charges. Ten days later, in a private ceremony, he was reinstated in the army. When he left the parade ground, Dreyfus was amazed to find hundreds of thousands of French people crying, "Long live justice."

Dreyfus fought valiantly in World War I; in September 1918, he was promoted to colonel and awarded the French Legion of Honor. He received a letter from Germany from Louise von Schwartzkoppen in June 1930: "Much esteemed Monsieur Dreyfus: I am mailing you under separate cover the diary of my late husband, General of the Infantry Max von Schwartzkoppen, published by Colonel Schwertfeger, and called *The Truth about Dreyfus.* I believe that I do this in the spirit of my husband whose wish has always been to testify in the monstrous trial of which you were the central figure and victim. For reasons that his memoirs clearly indicate, this was impossible for him to do."

*   *   *   *   *

Alfred Dreyfus, who was prejudged guilty merely because of his name, died after a lengthy illness in 1935. Anti-Semitism had cost France dearly. But *even before his death*, the same insidious pattern of hate, engulfing Christians as well as Jews, was beginning in neighboring Germany.

Unfortunately, it is a pattern that many fail to recognize in time. Such was the case among Christians in Hitler's Germany who refused to believe that the infamous "Nuremberg Laws" of 1935, which deprived Jews of their rights as German citizens, had anything to do with them.* The Vatican itself was led to believe that Hitler's anti-Semitic policies would not affect Catholics; however, the concordat guaranteeing freedom to the Church was not honored by Hitler. Catholic leaders were beaten, church property confiscated, priests killed.

In *Mein Kampf*, Hitler wrote "We must hold unflinchingly to our foreign policy, namely *to secure for the German people the land and soil to which they are entitled on this earth.* . . . Recognizing the necessity of a reckoning with France, it would remain ineffectual in the long view if it represented the whole of our aim . . . It can achieve meaning only if it offers the rear cover for an enlargement of our people's living space in Europe. The right to possess soil can become a duty. And most especially when not some little nigger nation or other is involved. . . . *It goes without saying that the Jews announce the sharpest resistance to such a policy.*"

An estimated fourteen million Christians fell prey to Hitler's policies. Yugoslavs, Czechs, Frenchmen, Norwegians, Danes, Poles, Dutchmen, Belgians, and Hungarians died in concentration camps or were forced into slave labor and worked to death in the fields and factories of the German Reich. Countless millions of Russians, Englishmen, and Americans were killed or maimed before Hitler's madness was finally halted.

Even after the passage of so many years we tend to defend

---

*Germany has had a long history of anti-Semitism. In the year 1298, one hundred thousand men, women, and children whose only sin was being born Jewish were hacked to death in Austria and southern Germany. They were accused of desecrating the host—pounding the wafer representing the body of Jesus into a blood-stained mass—in secret.

Centuries later, scientists discovered that the yellowish wafer kept in damp church cellars turned red because it developed a bacterial growth called Chromotbacterium prodigiosum, which is similar to streptomycetes, from which lifesaving antibiotics are extracted.

ourselves from the pain of coming to terms with the Holocaust by avoiding the subject altogether. Yet the following episode deserves your attention.

Rudolf Hoess supervised the Auschwitz concentration camp for a two month-period, during which time four hundred thousand Hungarian Jews were killed. He was condemned to death by a Polish court and hanged in 1947. Following is an excerpt from his autobiography, written while in prison.*

> They [the Jews] were taken from the detraining platform to the "Cottage"—across the meadows where Building Site II was located. On arrival at the "Cottage," they were told to undress. At first they went calmly into the rooms where they were supposed to be disinfected. But some of them showed signs of alarm, and spoke of death by suffocation and of annihilation. A sort of panic set in. Immediately all the Jews still outside were pushed into the chambers, and the doors were screwed shut. With subsequent transports the difficult individuals were picked out early on and most carefully supervised. At the first signs of unrest, those responsible were unobtrusively led behind the building and killed with a small-calibre gun that was inaudible to the others. I noticed that women who either guessed or knew what awaited them nevertheless found the courage to joke with the children to encourage them, despite the mortal terror visible in their own eyes.
>
> One woman approached me as she walked past and, pointing to her four children who were manfully helping the smallest ones over the rough ground, whispered:
>
> "How can you bring yourself to kill such beautiful, darling children? Have you no heart at all?"
>
> There were many such shattering scenes, which affected all who witnessed them.
>
> During the spring of 1942 hundreds of vigorous men and women walked all unsuspecting to their death in

---

*Rudolf Hoess, *Commandant of Auschwitz: An Autobiography*, translated by Constantine FitzGibbon (Cleveland: World Publishing Co., 1960).

the gas-chambers, under the blossom-laden fruit trees of the "Cottage" orchard. This picture of death in the midst of life remains with me to this day. . . .

I had to see everything, I had to watch hour after hour, by day and by night, the removal and burning of bodies, the extraction of the teeth, the cutting of hair, the whole grisly, interminable business. I had to stand for hours on end in the ghastly stench, while the mass graves were being opened and the bodies dragged out and burned.

I had to look through the peep-hole of the gas-chambers and watch the process of death itself, because the doctors wanted me to see it.

I always shuddered at the prospect of carrying out exterminations by shooting, when I thought of the vast numbers concerned, and of the women and children. I was therefore relieved to think that we were to be spared all these blood-baths. This caused me the greatest concern when I had heard Eichmann's description of Jews being mown down by the Special Squads (Einsatzkommandos) armed with machine-guns and machine-pistols. Many gruesome scenes are said to have taken place, people running away after being shot, the finishing off of the wounded and particularly of the women and children. Many members of the Einsatzkommandos, unable to endure wading through blood any longer, had committed suicide. Some had even gone mad. Most of the members of these Kommandos had to rely on alcohol when carrying out their horrible work. . . .

I had many detailed discussions with Eichmann concerning all matters connected with the "final solution of the Jewish problem," but without ever disclosing my inner anxieties, I tried in every way to discover Eichmann's innermost and real convictions about the "solution."

Yes, every way. Yet even when we were quite alone together and the drink had been flowing freely so that he was in his most expansive mood, he showed that he was completely obsessed with the idea of destroying every single Jew that he could lay his hands on. Without pity and in cold blood we must complete this extermination as rapidly as possible.

There was no escape for me from this dilemma.

I had to go on with this process of extermination. I had to continue this mass murder and coldly to watch it, without regard for the doubts that were seething deep inside me.

I had to observe every happening with a cold indifference. Even those petty incidents that others might not notice I found hard to forget.

Few today would deny a connection between this grisly series of events and anti-Semitism. Hitler may never have united Germany if he had not been able to capitalize on the average German's eagerness to blame Jews for all the country's ills.*

People remain surprisingly unaware of how easily an appeal to innate prejudice can lead to a breakdown of educational, individual, and social values. How tragic! When this takes place, the way is paved for the extermination of innocents, the entrapment of complacent bystanders, the engulfment of bigots themselves, and ultimately the destruction of entire civilizations.

Frustrated malcontents have always used scapegoats to compensate for their own baffling failures. Yet those who can least afford to do so are blinded to the danger of hate as a weapon that will be redirected toward themselves.

*In 1884, Sir William Osler, one of the great physicians of the nineteenth century, said, "Should another Moses arise and preach a Semitic exodus from Germany, and should he prevail, they would leave the land impoverished far more than ancient Egypt. . . . There is not a profession which would not suffer the serious loss of many of its most brilliant ornaments, and in none more so than in our own."

Osler's prophesy has come true. Although West Germany remains strong industrially, it can no longer claim first place in the realm of the intellect. For example, prior to World War II, we looked to Germany for leadership in ophthalmology, neurology, psychiatry, otology, and research against infectious diseases. Heretofore, before undertaking the study of medicine one had to be proficient in German. This no longer holds true.

"History repeats itself," Clarence Darrow once observed. "That's one of the things wrong with history."

•THE COST OF BIGOTRY•

The following article by Howard Vincent O'Brien is from the *Chicago Daily News,* June 27, 1938:

Pity the poor German!

If he has heart disease he can't use digitalis, because it was discovered by a Jew, Ludwig Traube.

If his tooth aches he cannot have the comfort of cocaine; for that would be utilizing the work of a Jew, Solomon Stricker.

He will find it hard to avoid typhus unless he takes advantage of what two Jews, Widal and Weil, learned about this disease.

If he has diabetes, the aid of insulin is not for him; for a Jew, Minkowski, had a hand in its discovery.

If he has a headache he must shun pyramidon and antipyris, discovered by the Jews Spiro and Filehne.

If his child has convulsions he must avoid chloral hydrate, the discovery of a Jew, Oscar Liebreich.

Misericordia!

Pity the poor German!

He must not even try to find whether he has syphilis, because the Wassermann reaction used for that purpose is the discovery of a Jew.

If he suspects he has gonorrhea he must not investigate because the method used is the discovery of a Jew, Neisser.

If he has a mental screw loose he must not attempt to tighten it by psychoanalysis, because the father of that technique is a Jew, Sigmund Freud.

Pity the poor German!

If he has ear trouble he can't go to Heinrich Neumann, the specialist who treated the Duke of Windsor. Professor Neumann is a Jew.

Pity the poor German!

If he has cancer he can get no help from the great specialist, Ferdinand Blumenthal. Professor Blumenthal has been forced to leave Germany.

If his wife needs the services of a gynecologist, she will have to consult somebody besides Drs. Bobl and Oscar Frankl. They have committed suicide. So has Dr. Knopfelmacher of Vienna. Well past seventy, this eminent scientist was "treated" with castor oil by patriotic Hitlerites.

Pity the poor German!

·10·

A REVERSAL OF DIRECTIONS

W hile in Rome, on a brilliant Sunday in 1962, my wife, Helen, decided that we should hasten to St. Peter's Basilica to hear Pope John present his Easter sermon. As we made our way through the silent throng, we realized how few Romans were present that morning; the faithful were mostly humble and deeply religious peasants who had come on foot or bicycle from the surrounding countryside. Others had arrived in bus caravans from as far away as Holland and Scandinavia.

The pope appeared on the balcony of St. Peter's, his vestments radiating the glory of the day for all believers. He began to speak, first in Italian, then in French, German, English—perhaps a dozen languages in all.

We were spellbound by his prodigious intelligence, transfigured by his expressions of love for all mankind, moved by his simplicity and lack of pretense.

Here was the man who swiftly and effectively reconciled Christianity to the teachings of Jesus by personally ordering certain phrases offensive to Jews stricken from the liturgy. Most important, Pope John believed the Second Vatican Council could provide an opportunity for the Catholic Church to repudiate traditions that too long had perpetuated hatred and oppression. Largely through his efforts, the highest ecclesiastical authorities of the Catholic Church committed themselves to uprooting the charge of collective guilt against the Jews, eliminating anti-Semitism, and fostering mutual respect and knowledge between Christians and Jews.

At an earlier stage in his career, Pope John had issued baptismal certificates to four thousand women and children to save them from Nazi extermination. This came about through the intervention of a concerned individual, Ira Hirschmann, who has since become a valued friend.

Ira was serving as President Franklin D. Roosevelt's special envoy to Turkey for the express purpose of saving lives. He learned that 516,000 Jews in Hungary had already been systematically slaughtered by the Nazis and that drastic measures were required if some of the remaining population were to be saved.

In desperation he turned to Gilbert Simond, the Catholic representative of the International Red Cross in Turkey, and asked if the Church could help.

Ira recollects Simond suggesting that "we meet with Monsignor Roncalli, the apostolic delegate of the Vatican and the pope's highest emissary in the Middle East. Soon we were on our way to a tiny island off the Dardanelles to meet with him."

As Ira remembers it, "A short, rotund man whose good humor was immediately evident in his eyes, twinkling under his black skullcap, he greeted us warmly and graciously welcomed us in Italian. The future Pope John listened intently as I outlined in halting Italian the perilous plight of the Jews remaining in Hungary. He then quietly asked, 'Do you have any contact with the underground in Hungary?' After I nodded yes he asked, 'Do you think that these Jews would undergo baptismal ceremonies?' 'If it meant saving their lives,' I replied, 'I think they would be ready to do so gratefully. I know what I would do,' I added.

"He said that he had reason to believe that the Nazis recognized baptismal certificates as credentials and permitted their holders to leave the country.

"We agreed that he would communicate with his representatives in Hungary and that I would get in touch with our underground connections to arrange a large-scale baptism of Jews with certificates to be issued to women and children. It would be up to those who were baptized to decide later whether they wished to remain in the Church or 'go their way.'

"Four thousand Hungarian Jews were saved thanks to the intervention of the benevolent apostolic delegate to the Middle East. No wonder I was moved to tears when in 1958 I learned that Angelo Roncalli had become Pope John XXIII."

Monsignor Roncalli's action was proof of his humane concern for the welfare of all humanity. Could any better example exist of the collaboration between a government's representative, who happened to be a Jew, and a compassionate agent of the Church?

Like Jesus, Pope John XXIII also stressed love and charity. He too was for inclusion, not exclusion. He too was tolerant and respectful of the dignity of all men. Prejudice was as foreign to his nature as sanctimonious piety, hollow ritual, and holier-than-thou posturings. Here was the man who thoroughly understood the morality of Jesus.

Angelo Roncalli's great achievement was to teach the world how small is hatred and how great is love. When he established the Ecumenical Council of Vatican II (1962–65) he proclaimed, "Now more than ever, certainly more than in the past centuries, our intention is to serve man as such and not only Catholics; to defend above all and everywhere the rights of the human person, and not only those of the Catholic Church."

* * * * *

The response to bigotry, to being excluded, is unpredictable. Some understandably shrink within themselves, fearful of further rebuffs. Others, insisting on constitutional rights, vigorously go on the offensive. Jewish and Christian theologians write learned tracts revealing the unreasonableness of prejudice.

I myself harbored feelings of resentment until I began to study the sources of anti-Semitism. Soon I came to the realization that an innocent child can learn racism and discrimination merely by imitating school friends or absorbing comments of parents.

Almost simultaneously, new vistas of appreciation opened up for me—an acknowledgment of the *positive,* constructive elements of all religions, all peoples. Many poignant episodes reinforced my feeling of liberation.

Some years ago my wife and I were driving through western England. Suddenly we saw in the distance the shimmering towers of a vast structure. As we came closer, its spires seemed to soar majestically toward the heavens.

We were looking at Wells Cathedral. Completed about 1300, it is second only to Canterbury in size and is equally beautiful. One hundred years of labor went into its construction. How amazing to suddenly see this demonstration of devotion rising precipitously from the flatlands of a tiny community of less than six thousand souls.

As I gazed at this triumph of Christianity, I couldn't help recalling the words of the renowned American physician and writer Oliver Wendell Holmes: "The stately synagogue should lift its walls by the side of the aspiring cathedral, a perpetual reminder that there are many mansions in the Father's earthly house as well as in the heavenly one; that *civilized humanity,* longer in time and broader in space than historical form of belief, is mightier than any one institution or organization it includes."

It often takes quite a while to civilize humanity. That was the experience of a man called Elias Bernstein, a recognized leader in his own community who was judged contemptuously by a stranger because of his name. But let me retrace for a moment.

My wife, Helen, and I had embarked on a ten-day trip through the highlands of Guatemala. We arrived rather late in the capital, Guatemala City, and retired almost immediately.

The members of our tour group assembled in the hotel lobby the following morning to be assigned to drivers. Two couples were delegated at random for each car, but, by chance, we were to travel alone. A Mr. and Mrs. "Jones" were teamed up with a Mr. and Mrs. Bernstein, who had not yet appeared. Vociferous objections arose from Mr. Jones. When I recovered from my initial shock, I announced that we would be delighted to share our car and driver with the Bernsteins.

The Bernsteins, it turned out, were a strikingly handsome couple. Gradually, the dominant figure of our journey became Elias Bernstein. His humor and humanity acted as a magnet that drew everyone to him from native children to his fellow travelers.

Something astonishing happened at our group's farewell dinner, where Mr. Bernstein had been given the seat of honor. After final farewells and toasts had been offered, Mr. Jones arose from his seat, walked slowly and deliberately across the room, and stood directly in front of the man with whom he had refused to associate. He extended his hand and said, loudly enough for all to hear, "Will you please forgive me? The only time I didn't like you was when I didn't know you."

Mr. Bernstein shook his hand warmly.

* * * * *

"As a crowd huddled under leaden skies, Rabbi Ira J. Rothstein began scrubbing—slowly, then more vigorously—to erase the swastikas and other anti-Semitic graffiti from a wall of the Beth Shalom Synagogue.

"Standing shoulder to shoulder with the rabbi, the Reverend Robert Wozniak, pastor of St. Robert Bellarmine Roman Catholic church here, said, 'I'm happy it's getting off—I only wish we could erase it from people's hearts as easily.' "*

It was 1984 and vandals had desecrated a beautiful new synagogue just completed in Manalapan Township, New Jersey. In an extemporaneous display of unity and sympathy, church leaders and a thousand people, including New Jersey's Governor Kean, had gathered in the high school football field nearby and then marched to the new building to remove the slogans of hatred.

Governor Kean, addressing the crowd, said, "Your public solidarity is the firmest defense of all of us against discrimination and bigotry." Catholic and Protestant clergy gave sermons denouncing this loathsome sacrilege. James Davis, an Episcopalian seminary graduate who came to scrub the offending scrawls from the wall with his three children, said, "You have to start with the children. You have to show that there are a lot of people who show care and respect for other people."

Another resident, Donald Walker, who was there with his son Jeffrey, said, "I couldn't really believe that people hate that much." Robert Connolly, there with his son Adam, said, "I want to teach him that hatred and violence are not acceptable."

Father Wozniak proclaimed, "I hope that when we leave

*From a *New York Times* article by James Brook, 5 November 1984.

this field we don't forget . . . that we can't wish prejudice away. We can't pray it away. It will only go away when we work at it."

* * * * *

At an interfaith meeting, I met Rabbi Marc Tanenbaum, recognized internationally as an outstanding ecumenical scholar. Working with him, I grew to learn the thinking of many Christian leaders who were his friends—Father Edward Flannery, Sister Rose Thiering, Bishop Paul Moore, Jr., Billy Graham, Cardinal Joseph Bernardin, Archbishop Jean Jabot, and Father Theodore Hesburgh.

Each of these prominent representatives of Christianity has tried to accentuate similarities between religions and reduce tensions created by negative teachings. In the same spirit, Christian scholars have begun questioning the Gospel account of the death of Jesus by taking the position that the Gospels are theological interpretations, all of which contain at least some incidents that could not have actually occurred.

From the Roman Catholic archdiocese of Cincinnati comes this statement: "The Jewish people is not collectively guilty of the passion and death of Jesus Christ, nor of the rejection of Jesus as Messiah. The Jewish people is not damned, nor bereft of its election. Their suffering, dispersion, and persecution are not punishments for the Crucifixion or the rejection of Jesus." This new approach was confirmed at a recent meeting of the Synod of Bishops when Cardinal Roger Etchegaray of Marseilles stated, "During this synod my thoughts have gone out particularly to the Jewish people. For it is indeed that people which, of all peoples, ought to be the first beneficiary of the church's twofold mission of reconciliation and penance, in properly religious consideration of the fact of the original bond linking Judaism and Christianity."

The germs of anti-Semitism within the Lutheran faith are repudiated in the following statement by representatives of the Lutheran World Federation in Stockholm, Sweden, July 11–13, 1983: ". . . the deplorable religious anti-Semitism of the 16th century, to which Luther's attacks made important contribution, is a horrible anachronism when translated to the conditions of the modern world. . . . To their credit it is to be said that there were individuals and groups among Lutherans who in defiance of totalitarian power defended their Jewish neighbors, both in Germany and elsewhere. . . . Lutherans of today refuse to be bound by all of Luther's utterances on the Jews. We hope we have learned from the tragedies of the recent past."

And this from a United Methodist document: "Jews . . . have been victims of systematic oppression and injustice. . . . Therefore, in order to continue Jewish and Christian efforts for the common cause of mankind, it is not enough for contemporary Christians to be aware of our common origins. Christians must also become aware of that history in which they have deeply alienated the Jews. They are obligated to examine their own implicit and explicit responsibility for the discrimination against and for organized extermination of Jews, as in the recent past. The persecution by Christians of Jews throughout the centuries calls for clear repentance and resolve to repudiate past injustice and to seek its elimination in the present."

In 1970, a penetrating statement was issued by the Vatican Secretariat for Promoting Christian Unity, excerpts of which follow:

> It is in "searching into the mystery of the Church" itself (*Nostra Aetate*) that the Council was led to recall the bond that unites the Christian people to the descendants of Abraham. The Declaration published on that occasion is a document that inaugurates a new era

in the relations of Christians and Jews. The heritage of the past, it is true, still weighs heavily on these relations. But in the light of the clear affirmations of the Council, all Christians are called to an effort of comprehension and searching, which ought to translate itself into action in order that this document should not remain a dead letter. . . .

The New Testament itself affirms the permanent value of the *Sacred Books* on which the faith of the Jewish people is founded and from which it is nourished. "Think not that I have come to abolish the law and the Prophets; I have come not to abolish them but to fulfill them" (Mt. 5:17); "to them belong the sonship, the glory, the covenants, the giving of the law, the worship and the promises; to them belong the patriarchs . . ." (Rom. 9:4); the Jews "are beloved for the sake of their forefathers. For the gifts and the call of God are irrevocable" (Rom. 11:28–29).

The Church is not born solely of scripture but also of the living tradition of the Jewish people. Providence has not limited itself to a "simple bookish preparation of the coming of the Messiah" (L. Bouyer, *La Bible et L'Evangile*, 2, 248). Christ, His apostles, and the first Christians participated in this tradition. "As transforming as Christian revelation may be, it is from the Jewish tradition that it draws not only its formulas, its images, its setting, but even the marrow of its concepts" (ibid., 250). Christianity, on the other hand, is not bound directly to the Old Testament as such, but rather as it was interpreted by the ancient Jewish tradition.*

A detailed interfaith statement concerning the Christian-Jewish dialogue was issued by the Executive Committee of the World Council of Churches at Geneva on July 16, 1982. Following are excerpts from a lengthy series of "guidelines":

Information Service No. 9, February 1970/1, of the Secretariat for Promoting Christian Unity.

... when the words of Jesus came to be used by Christians who did not identify with the Jewish people as Jesus did, [his] sayings often became weapons in anti-Jewish polemics and thereby their original intention was tragically distorted. An internal Christian debate is now taking place on the question of how to understand passages in the New Testament that seem to contain anti-Jewish references. . . . Teachings of contempt for Jews and Judaism in certain Christian traditions proved a spawning ground for the evil of the Nazi Holocaust. The Church must learn so to preach and teach the Gospel as to make sure that it cannot be used towards contempt for Judaism and against the Jewish people. A further response to the Holocaust by Christians, and one which is shared by their Jewish partners, is a resolve that it will never happen again to the Jews or to any other people.

Within this context, brotherhood between Christians and Jews can have deeper significance for us if we recall the words of the eminent French historian Julian Green, who wrote several decades ago:

There is no escaping the fact we Christians are almost all responsible in degrees which vary mysteriously from one soul to the next, according to our capacity for understanding; and Jesus' passion continues to be acted out night and day in the world. . . . We cannot raise our hands against a Jew without striking with the same blow him who is the man par excellence and, at the same time, the flower of Israel; and it is Jesus who suffered in the concentration camps; it is always he, his suffering is never ended. Ah, to be done with all this, and to begin all over again! To meet on the morning of the Resurrection and to clasp Israel to our hearts, weeping, without a word. For after Auschwitz, only tears can have meaning. Christian, wipe the tears and the blood from the face of your Jewish brother, and the countenance of your Christ will shine upon you both.

Today it is neither necessary nor desirable for Christians to look upon Jews as outsiders. Rather, it is time for both religions, one huge and powerful, the other proud and time-honored, to reach out in friendship toward goals of common understanding. This need not result in diminishing the distinctiveness of either Christianity or Judaism. On the contrary, both religions can be strengthened through such efforts by creating bonds of understanding.

To do so will not be easy, for Christians have been indoctrinated from generation to generation to look upon Jews as an example of what *not* to be. Yet if one embraces the basic Judeo-Christian philosophy of "love thy neighbor as thyself," one will be willing to reexamine and rethink those early teachings in order to move closer to Jesus, for whom prejudice was an unknown emotion.

Ecumenical meetings and dialogues between ministers of all faiths are invaluable, a radical and desirable breach of former rigidly held attitudes. Relaying themes of tolerance to all peoples, however, remains a problem.

There may be a simple, effective means of accomplishing that purpose. At least once a month, regularly, from every Christian pulpit, a message could go forth: "Jesus Christ, our Lord, was a Jew. If you revere him, you must excise bigotry from your heart."

What better time to resolutely emphasize Jesus' plea for love, peace, and healing than Christmas, the day of his birth. Yet, in one city, New York, the city with the largest Jewish population in the world, the *New York Times'* condensation of sermons of ten leading priests and ministers on Christmas Day 1984 contained no mention whatever that the holiday being celebrated was in honor of a Jew—Jesus Christ.

Although the Reverend Arthur N. Pappas, pastor of the Greek
Orthodox Church of the Annunciation in Manhattan, did
observe:

> In Bethlehem where the Word became flesh, the Chris-
> tian churches vie for the privileges of the Shrine of the
> Nativity. Where we long for fraternity, we find bigotry.
> In place of harmony, we encounter dissension. Where
> we anticipate agape, we are appalled to uncover hatred.
>
> Each Christian church prides itself in holding its
> own Nativity service, leaving the impression that the
> King of Kings was born in Bethlehem for their followers
> alone. This approach simply widens the chasm be-
> tween the Christians and does not advance the message
> of peace that His birth presaged or alleviate the prej-
> udice He came to abolish.
>
> Christmas should imply the mass or the liturgy of
> Emmanuel for all people, regardless of color or ethnic
> background. The Apostles preached "to all nations,"
> commanding them to repent and accept the Savior of
> the world.
>
> Let's celebrate Christmas this year in the spirit of
> reconciliation to one another. The rich empathizing
> with the poor; the strong reinforcing the weak; the
> lovely embracing the unlovely, and the Orthodox,
> Catholic, and Protestant Christians welcoming one an-
> other with the kiss of peace.

No one could disagree with this strong appeal to reconcile
all branches of Christianity. By omission, however, even
this sermon, which pleads tolerance, illustrates how little
importance is attached to alleviating prejudice against Jews.

Interreligious bigotry will forever be perpetuated unless
the true relationship of Jesus to his people is revealed over
and over again.

If it were possible for Christians and Jews to receive a
message from Jesus, it would be clear and uncompromising:
look after the poor, the destitute, the afflicted and under-

privileged; commit yourself to repudiating religious, racial, and political bigotry wherever it exists, now and forever. Commit yourself to a policy of compassion. Rid yourself of feelings of hostility and find a way toward mutual trust. Jesus would embrace peoples crushed under dictatorships, Palestinians suffering in their refugee camps, Israelis tormented by internationalized prejudice, blacks deprived of social justice.

We must heed that dictum. We cannot afford to fail.

A timely story from a church text, *The Pearl and the Seed*, illustrates how compassionate Christian leaders are confronting prejudice and helping change attitudes.

Bishop Bernard Sheil of Chicago, founder of the Catholic Youth Organization, delivered an unpopular sermon some years ago. His subject, the Jewish heritage of Mary and Jesus. Amid the derision, a woman planted herself in front of the Bishop and shrilled, "You're not a Catholic, you're a Rabbi."

Bishop Sheil quietly replied, "I thank you, madam, for the compliment. Rabbi? That's what they called our Lord."

·11·

BROTHERHOOD IN DEED

George Washington said, "The citizens of the United States of America have a right to applaud themselves for having given to mankind examples of an enlarged and liberal policy, a policy worthy of imitation.

"May the children of the stock of Abraham who dwell in this land continue to merit and enjoy the goodwill of the other inhabitants, while everyone shall sit in safety under his own vine and fig tree and there shall be none to make him afraid."

Many Americans have tacitly accepted the wisdom of our first president. Some, however, have gone out of their way to support the principle of a pluralistic society by actively participating in non-Christian causes.

Such a man is Warren Eustis, a friend who lives in Minneapolis, Minnesota. Warren, a white Anglo-Saxon Protestant attorney, has not exactly led an easy life. He has fought and won an extended battle against alcoholism, is now combating bone cancer, and spends every free moment with his wife, Nancy, who was in a car accident that left her permanently paralyzed.

Nothing has fazed Warren. He became the first president of the Minnesota Chemical Dependency Association, founded a home to help cure youthful drug users, and was elected president of his local bar association.

In the spring of 1984, Warren was approached by Samuel Heller, executive director of the Jewish National Fund (JNF). He had never heard of it. Upon inquiry, he found that its purpose was to reclaim land and plant trees in Israel as well as send afforestation experts to underdeveloped countries to push back the deserts and create viable agricultural and economic bases for their peoples.

The JNF wanted Warren to become chairman of a fund-raising dinner. He accepted and named Peter Dorsey, another WASP, as his co-chairman. They decided that they would ask the exclusive Minneapolis Club for its cooperation. They agreed that helping Israel would be proper and desirable, and a steering committee was formed consisting principally of club members.

On August 23, 1984, at the Radisson South Hotel in Minneapolis, four hundred people, mostly Christians, set a new record for money raised in the Midwest on behalf of the Jewish National Fund.

Warren's comment to me: "It was fun."

* * * * *

Born directly opposite Abraham Lincoln's house in Springfield, Illinois, Julius Rosenwald must have been deeply influenced by "Honest Abe's" character.

Early in his career, Rosenwald joined Sears, Roebuck and Company. Sensing the potential of mail order sales, he built the struggling young firm into a giant corporation respected worldwide for its integrity and sound business practices.

His business achievements notwithstanding, Rosenwald is best remembered for his munificent acts of philanthropy. "It is unselfish effort, helpfulness to others, that ennobles life," he once said, "not because of what it does for others but more what it does for ourselves. In this spirit, we should give not grudgingly, but gladly, generously, eagerly, lovingly, joyfully, indeed with the supreme pleasure that life can furnish."

The Musuem of Science and Industry in Chicago was founded by Rosenwald. He helped organize the Municipal Voters League, was the guiding light of the Chicago Planning Commission, and supported the University of Chicago with gifts of more than five million dollars. He helped to build educational facilities in Turkey and set up feeding stations and dental clinics in Germany after World War I.

A champion of the underprivileged, Rosenwald did more to improve black education than any other white person in private life. In 1913, there was not one standard elementary school for blacks in the South, and of course no high school. In the same year, Rosenwald set up a fund to construct black educational facilities. Twenty years later, there were 5,357 "Rosenwald" schools in existence in 15 states and 883 counties, with nearly 15,000 teachers instructing 650,000 black children.

Rockefeller and Ford may have given away more; but, neither used his wealth more intelligently or more imaginatively than Julius Rosenwald.

* * * * *

Throughout the centuries, Holy Week, particularly Good Friday, which recalls the crucifixion of Jesus, has provoked pogroms and mass slayings of Jews. Some of these ancient prejudices are dissolving as Christian theologians delve more deeply into Jesus' unshakable connection with his Jewish brethren. The Second Vatican Council, which disavowed anti-Semitism and repudiated the slander that the Jews were guilty of the death of Jesus, helped stir an awakened spirit of brotherhood.

More and more Christians, for example, want to experience the Passover seder (the Last Supper), as Jesus did.

On April 19, 1984, Auxiliary Bishop Eugene Marino conducted an interreligious Holy Thursday mass commemorating the Last Supper in Washington, D.C. "We are very conscious that the roots of our faith are in the Jewish tradition," said the Reverend Sean O'Malley as he welcomed Jewish visitors to the mass.

Later the same day, the interfaith group gathered to celebrate a Passover seder at the B'nai B'rith headquarters.

Father Lori, who has participated in previous Passover celebrations elsewhere, commented, "The symbols of Jewish rituals should be familiar to Catholics because there is no other way to understand the Eucharist as a memorial of the great deeds of redemption without returning to the Jewish ritual meals of which the seder is the example par excellence." He continued, "Then, too, our notion of the Eucharist as a memorial of the death and resurrection of Jesus is rooted in the Jewish concept of the memorial of the first Exodus. So we have come to interpret Jesus' passage from death to life as a new and definitive Exodus, one that we shall all have to make."

The similarity of elements within the mass and seder surprised Christians and Jews alike at these interreligious services. A number mentioned that the raising and the blessing of the wafer at the mass was comparable to the raising and the blessing of the unleavened bread at the seder. Others were struck with the community of interests found in the rituals. All were impressed with the knowledge that this period of the year historically was a time for hostility, which is now being reversed in deed.

In keeping with these new attitudes, the Vatican Secretariat for Promoting Christian Unity urged the following:

> Recent research by liturgists has come to the conclusion that in order fully to understand Christian tradition and institutions, it is *indispensable* to examine Jewish institutions themselves in depth. This is particularly clear in the case of the origin of the sacra-

ments. Christians have adopted the Jewish feasts and prayers, adapting them to the Revelation brought by Christ. Their fundamental meaning, however, can be grasped only by constant reference to the original milieu. But the Jewish liturgy is still celebrated today in the same terms as in the ancient period when the first Christians participated in it. What more suggestive way is there to understand the institution of the Eucharist in the setting of the Jewish Passover meal than the Passover Seder *in a Jewish family!**

* * * * *

The preliminary xeroxing for this manuscript was done in a small shop by a young Hispanic working for a Hasidic Jew. In the course of this work I came in contact with them frequently and gradually became aware of a remarkable father-son relationship.

The young man, I learned, came from a broken home, had very little formal education, no friends, and not much hope for advancement on his own.

As breadwinner for a growing family, the Jewish owner has more than his share of anxiety. Yet I noticed him going out of his way to help his young assistant, who is now being taught how to keep records, maintain a filing system, and control inventory.

On my last visit I learned that the young assistant is now going to night school at the suggestion, and with the support of, his employer, who surely must realize that his assistant will soon go on to a better job.

Imagine the difficulty of two people from entirely different cultures communicating with one another, for neither speaks much English. Yet they manage with a common language of concern and mutual respect.

*Information Service No. 9, February 1970/1, of the Secretariat for Promoting Christian Unity.

* * * * *

A Jewish volunteer worker at the North Shore University Hospital in Manhasset, Long Island, noticed that a number of Christian volunteers and staff members were distressed at having to work on the Christmas holiday. She called Samuel Baker at Temple Beth El in Great Neck. On short notice, he enlisted the aid of fourteen volunteers to substitute for Christian hospital workers.

That was twelve years ago. Since then, every year at the Christmas season Jewish volunteers have filled in for the Christian staff. The group now numbers over one hundred people.

Today, two other synagogues provide volunteers for St. Francis Hospital and the Veterans Hospital on the North Shore of Long Island. A synagogue on the South Shore is planning a similar program with the encouragement and assistance of the Long Island Federation of Temple Brotherhoods.

Volunteers man the Emergency Room and nursing stations, bring meals, and comfort patients. They gather up and assist nonambulatory patients so they can attend the special Christmas mass at St. Francis Hospital.

Carol Hauptmann, in the Community Relations Department of the hospital, said to me, "My Christian co-workers are so delighted with this project that two years ago they organized a similar program to take Jewish patients down to Yom Kippur services. We believe it to be a unique program that should be implemented by all the other hospitals."

* * * * *

In private clubs, discrimination based on religion is an exclusionary practice that perpetuates prejudice; it is particularly painful to people of the Jewish faith.

Westchester is a suburban county just north of New York

City, with a population of a million people. Twenty years ago, its thirty-seven private golf clubs were exclusively Christian or Jewish.

An event of some significance occurred about that time and changed attitudes dramatically. The daughter of a Christian club member invited a young Jewish guest to be her escort at a dance. He was asked to leave, and his humiliation was duly recored in all Westchester County newspapers. The minister of a local church was shocked, and in his sermon the following Sunday he sadly observed, "If Jesus Christ were to return to earth tomorrow, he would not be allowed to enter the dining room of the _____Golf Club."

The good Scarsdale pastor must have realized that ejecting a decent young man solely because of his Jewish heritage not only defames Jesus, but his mother Mary, Joseph, Saint Peter, Saint Paul, Saint Thomas, Saints Matthew, Mark, and John (compilers of the Gospels) and all the other Jewish founders of Christianity.

Unfortunately, maligning Jews seems to be par for the course in many club locker rooms. While reinforcing feelings of superiority and exclusivity, this practice continues to perpetuate, perhaps unthinkingly, the slanderous myths, catchwords, and shibboleths of the past.

In a complete reversal, the country club located in Scarsdale has now opened its doors to Jewish members, as have many other "Christian" clubs in the area.

The Westchester Seniors Golf Association has been a major ecumenical force in this transformation. Its 360 members, all over the age of fifty-five, recruited from every country club in the county, represent a happy example of democracy in action. Meeting three times a year for tournaments followed by cocktails and dinner, the conviviality of this group is genuine and heartwarming. Dozens of new friendships have resulted. People are learning that differences dissolve with close association.

·12·

DEFUSING DIFFERENCES

For centuries, dissimilarities between Christianity and Judaism made it impossible to realize the dream of the brotherhood of man. Christianity was based on the divinity of Christ; Jews believed in the absolute humanity of Jesus. These ideological differences were exacerbated over the centuries by political and psychological complications.

Today, differences between Christians and Jews are being diminished by a shared American way of life increasingly important in determining what we think and feel. All religious institutions have had to adjust to this reality by focusing on major issues that transcend sectarian considerations, such as nuclear disarmament, random violence, racial injustice, poverty, women's rights, drugs, pornography, and sexual mores. What has resulted are divisions and distinctions within religious denominations that are determined not so much by theological considerations as by social, cultural, economic, and educational background.

Living as we do under such conditions, Christians and Jews have far more in common today than ever before in their long and often tragic history. Every day millions of Christians and Jews watch the same basketball and baseball games, seek professional advice for similar problems, enter military service, go to doctors, and enter hospitals irrespective of their religious beliefs.

The role played by museums, theaters, and concert halls in our society makes the areas of commonality between people of differing faiths far greater than in past centuries, when art forms were as distinct from one another as the religions that fostered them.

Art transcends religious distinctions. I recall being seated next to a priest at a performance of a Sean O'Casey play some years ago. We were both moved to tears. We started a conversation during the intermission and I learned that he was a graduate of Holy Cross from Boston. Over coffee after the show we found that our emotional responses to the drama we had seen were almost identical, even though we had come from such different backgrounds. You don't have to be Irish to enjoy Sean O'Casey any more than you have to be Jewish to relate to *Fiddler on the Roof*.

That message was brought home to me when my wife and I were vacationing in Scotland. We were invited to a hotel in Edinburgh for a birthday celebration, and much to our surprise heard the familiar strains of "If I Were a Rich Man." Heading in that direction, we entered a ballroom to discover an amazing sight—scores of elegant Scotsmen dressed in kilts, dancing with their partners to a melody derived from a Yiddish folk song. Two very different ethnic cultures brought closer together by music.

Especially in America, far fewer barriers exist between a Christian and a Jew of similar social standing than between, say, a cab driver and an Ivy League executive of the same faith. A Christian nowadays would not feel particularly out of place at a colleague's Chanukah celebration or a Jewish wedding ceremony.

One reason for this is our tendency to stress areas of common interest and need regarding even our most important religious celebrations. Thus, Christmas and Chanukah have become occasions for people of all faiths to express a sense of cheer and goodwill irrespective of religious distinctions.

This is not to say that a Jew can ever feel what a Christian experiences in celebrating the birth of his Lord, any more than a Christian can become one with a Jew in celebrating God's ongoing commitment to his Chosen People. Rather, it is merely to acknowledge the capacity of Christians and Jews in America to respect each other's opinions and beliefs to the extent of hearing the voice of a common God who calls us all to come to Him by whatever path we choose.

That common voice was heard over three hundred years ago by the Puritans who founded this country. Though intolerant of other religions, they modeled themselves after biblical heroes and found parallels between incidents in their own lives and events in the Old Testament.

They even went so far as to draw an analogy between their flight from despotic Europe to America and the exodus of the Jews from Egypt. William Bradford, the first governor of Plymouth Colony, talked and wrote repeatedly about a covenant between the colonists and God much like the ancient biblical covenant with the Almighty.

Many of the early Puritan ministers mastered Hebrew sufficiently to speak it with ease. Their children were given Hebrew names—Sarah, Eliezer, Ezra, Abraham, Moses. Towns were also given ancient Hebrew names—Canaan, Goshen, Hebron, Sharon, Salem.

The Puritans modeled their celebrations of the Sabbath after Jewish customs. The first book published in America was the Bay Psalm Book, a direct translation of the Hebrew Book of Psalms.

* * * * *

It is important in this age of ecumenism for both Christians and Jews to look upon one another in an affirmative light. In order to do so, the New Testament cannot be viewed by Christians as a replacement of God's original covenant with his Chosen People, but rather as an outgrowth of the ancient root of Judaism with the power to add new dimensions to the central core of Christianity.

The Right Reverend Paul Moore, Jr., Episcopal bishop of New York, affirms this: "I see the Old Covenant and the New as different yet complementary ways to serve our mutual Lord."

Likewise, Jews have reason to be grateful to Christianity for carrying their message of justice and love to the four corners of the world. The Old Testament has been translated by Christians into more than a thousand languages and dialects. This most likely would not have happened were it not for their belief in Jesus as "a light for revelation to the Gentiles and for glory to thy people Israel" (Luke 2:32).

Bishop John Shelby Spong, of the Episcopal diocese of Newark, New Jersey, acclaims, "I cannot worship the Christ who fulfilled every human aspiration without also embracing the world gladly; . . . I cannot stand in awe of the freedom and wholeness in this Christ and not seek to break every tie which binds me or any other human being into anything less than full humanity. My worship demands that I be willing to contend against the prejudice, bigotry, fear, or whatever else wraps and denies another's personhood. Worship of this Christ is thus for me a call to life, to love, to compassion, to sensitivity and to the quest of justice. It is a call to the risks of involvement and confrontation with every human being."

·13·

THE JEWISH CONNECTION

During the course of seeking new insights into the historical Jesus, you have encountered Jewish people with whom you have had no personal identification.

In subsequent chapters, however, you will discover many Jews with whom you already have a cordial acquaintanceship and experience a warm kinship.

They have entertained generations of Americans; created music and works of art universally admired; won Nobel Prizes for developing antibiotics, polio vaccines, and other lifesaving medical miracles; helped in founding our most prestigious institutions; led in battle, and made sacrifices for their country.

Many have changed their names without in any way altering their religious beliefs. "Few Christians, while deploring open anti-Semitism, are aware of the subtle form it takes in our society," says Dr. Arnold Theodore Olson, president emeritus of the Evangelical Free Church of America. He continues, "No wonder many [Jews] seek to hide their Jewish identity in a society where the rest of us without\ fear almost flaunt our background."

These extraordinary men and women are neither alien, strange, or different, nor in any way opposed to the values Christians cherish most. Their goals are similar; they are just as capable of love and despair, of contributing to and sharing in the joys and rewards of living in a free society. They are no less American than Stephen Foster, Mark Twain, or Alexander Hamilton (who had a Jewish stepmother).

What is significant about the fact that these people share a Jewish background?

First, it would seem that Jews are accepted as cultural heroes by millions of people of varying religious backgrounds.

Second, there is a vast difference between the perception of "Jews" in the abstract and real life men and women.

Third, I am not suggesting that any one religious group is composed solely of talented persons. In our day to day existence, Jews are no better or worse than others. And, physically, not all Jews resemble Paul Newman or Paulette Goddard any more than all Christians compare favorably with Robert Redford or the late Marilyn Monroe. The human form comes in all shapes and sizes.

Finally, those with exceptional gifts portrayed in succeeding pages merely prove that it is not the label but the individual that counts.

In every thoughtful Christian life, there should be a Jesus connection and a corresponding Jewish connection.

*   *   *   *   *

Did you know that the music and lyrics of "White Christmas," "God Bless America," and "Easter Parade" were written by a Jew respectful of Christianity and grateful to America? Of course, it was Irving Berlin.

Are you aware that Rodgers and Hart, Bob Dylan, Eugene Ormandy, Dinah Shore, Arthur Fiedler, Eddy Duchin, Billy Joel, and Victor Borge share the same heritage?

When you have seen a film starring Kirk Douglas, Lauren Bacall, or Paul Newman, turned on television to William Shatner as Captain Kirk and Leonard Nimoy as Mr. Spock in "Star Trek," Lorne Greene in "Bonanza," or Michael

Landon in "Little House on the Prairie," did you realize that all these people are Jewish?

There are many more, like Cary Grant and the late Douglas Fairbanks, with one Jewish parent. Whatever the field—Fiorello LaGuardia in politics, Jonas Salk in medicine, or Admiral Hyman Rickover, father of the nuclear submarine—dedicated Jews have influenced your life in remarkable ways.

· SCIENCE AND MEDICINE ·

Undoubtedly, the most noted Jew of our time, one whose ideas have affected us profoundly, was *Albert Einstein* (1879–1955). His theory of relativity, using time and space in one unitary principle, has forever superseded all past concepts in the physical sciences, altered the course of international events and political action, and even changed the way we think about the future.

Einstein was shocked when his famous equation $E = mc^2$ was demonstrated in the most terrifying way by the bombs that destroyed Hiroshima and Nagasaki. For a long time he could only utter, "Horrible, horrible."

A deeply religious man, Einstein was convinced that "the less knowledge a scholar possesses, the farther he feels from God. But the greater his knowledge, the nearer his approach to God."

Almost as world-shaking was research on human behavioral patterns done by *Sigmund Freud* (1856–1939). It revolutionized the often brutal treatment of mentally disturbed people. When at the age of thirty-nine Freud first used the term "psychoanalysis," he was already well on his way to discovering that the dreams of every person serve as a "royal road" to the unconscious.

No longer could civilized people look upon themselves as primarily rational beings. For Freud had shown man to be a creature whose mind was largely at the mercy of forces unknown to him.

Far from diminishing our capacity for freedom, however, Freud's findings were instrumental in alleviating certain forms of nervous disorders that had hitherto been thought incurable. By showing that the same fundamental processes were at work among all people regardless of whether they were classified as normal or neurotic, Freud paved the way for the removal of moral and social stigma from mental illness.

Freud and Einstein were giants who literally changed our world But their awesome achievements cannot diminish the contributions of the many scientists and doctors who have done so much to prolong our lives. They have helped to decrease infant mortality rate and dramatically improve the quality of life by providing us with new diagnostic techniques and miraculous pharmaceuticals.

Selman A. Waksman (1888–1973) will be celebrated in the annals of medical history as the scientist who spent a lifetime of research on soil biology and after forty years discovered the powerful lifesaving antibiotic streptomycin.

Experimenting with thousands of bacterial strains, he finally found a form of actinomycetes that would provide a potent weapon against harmful bacteria without exerting deleterious effects on human beings. He was awarded a Nobel Prize in physiology and medicine in 1952.

Another formidable achievement, heralded as one of the greatest breakthroughs in medical history, was accomplished through a series of complex experiments leading to the discovery of an enzyme, DNA, which, in the presence of a template, can reproduce an exact copy of the original molecule. Through his years of research, Dr. *Arthur Kornberg* (1918–   ) has brought us significantly closer to discovering the secret of life itself. Scientists may soon be able to influence and actually alter basic hereditary characteristics.

Biochemist Kornberg was awarded a Nobel Prize for this incredible development called "genetic control."

Dr. *Jonas Salk* (1914–   ) was the first person to discover a vaccine for the prevention of poliomyelitis, a disease that, in this century alone, has claimed hundreds of thousands of lives.

Choosing himself, his wife, and his three sons as subjects for the first experimental injections in 1954, Salk subsequently turned over the new vaccine to the National Foundation for Infantile Paralysis for testing on nearly 1 million children. Reports showing the vaccine to be both effective and safe led to its official licensing the following year.

Though now largely augmented by a live virus developed by Dr. Albert Sabin, Salk's discovery was nonetheless the most important single development in the eradication of all forms of poliomyelitis, both paralytic and nonparalytic, from the United States.

If you needed a transfusion recently and did not contract hepatitis, then you may want to thank *Rosalyn Yalow* (1921–   ), a physicist who, with Dr. S. A. Berson, invented a screening technique now used in blood banks everywhere that is one hundred times more effective than anything previously used.

An entire range of illnesses can be diagnosed for subsequent treatment through the RIA kits Yalow helped to develop in order to ascertain the amount of biological and pharmacological substances in the blood and tissues of the body.

Scientists and physicists have applauded Yalow for not patenting the results of her remarkable breakthrough, but instead placing them in the public domain.

For her tremendous achievements, Rosalyn Yalow became the second woman in the history of medicine to receive a Nobel Prize, thus making her childhood dream of emulating Madame Curie come true.

Best known as the person who synthesized DNA, the genetic blueprint, in a test tube, and RNA, the messenger that delivers the DNA information, *Solomon Spiegelman* (1914–   ), as director of Columbia University's Institute of Cancer Research, has saved countless lives through his research. His work has made it possible to examine human cancers for possible viral agents. As a result, in the field of cancer prevention and therapy, there are better prospects today for a direct attack on cancer than ever before.

Erik H. Erikson (1902–   ), who coined the expression "identity crisis," is one of today's foremost psychoanalysts. Erikson believes that we undergo a crisis in each phase of maturation even though our personalities are formed permanently very early in life.

These views were reinforced during his treatment of emotionally disturbed veterans of World War II in San Francisco. He believed they were not mentally ill but were undergoing excruciating problems of adjustment that would trouble any normal person.

Erikson himself had his own identity crisis. Born of Danish parents in Frankfurt, Germany, he had a mixed background. The chief rabbi of Stockholm was a forebear on his mother's side. His father was a Protestant. Erikson thought of himself as a German of Danish heritage but was taunted by anti-Semitic German schoolmates and not fully accepted at the synagogue because of his Scandinavian appearance.

Joshua Lederberg (1925–   ) received a Nobel Prize in physiology and medicine "for his discoveries concerning genetic recombination and the organization of the genetic material of bacteria." Before Dr. Lederberg's experiments, it was widely believed that bacteria reproduced by simple cell division; but by 1947, Lederberg showed conclusively "that bacteria . . . reproduce by the union of two organisms with a consequent exchange of genes."

The importance of Dr. Lederberg's discovery, according

to the *New York Times,* may in time make "even the discovery of atomic energy . . . seem relatively small." This becomes increasingly apparent as greater knowledge of genetics brings us closer to a cure for cancer.

Almost as spectacular as our progress in the healing sciences are innovative ideas for products as disparate as submarines and cameras, which have strengthened America militarily and economically.

In June 1952, President Truman lauded the U.S.S. *Nautilus,* saying, "The day the propellers of this new submarine first bite into the water . . . will be the most momentous day in atomic science since that first flash in the desert seven years ago."

Polish-born Rear Admiral *Hyman Rickover* (1900–   ) accomplished this most important development in naval history by resorting to unconventional production methods that shocked top brass—especially when captains were told to take orders from noncommissioned seamen.

Rickover deplores government debt and waste, declaring, "If the Russians announced today that they were going to send a man to hell, there would be at least two government agencies asking for money tomorrow on the grounds that we should get there first."

The most imaginative naval officer in recent history, Admiral Rickover not only developed underwater ships, but also atomic-powered aircraft carriers, infrared signaling, underwater detectors, a specialized mine sweeper, and shock-proof electrical equipment aboard warships.

On a vacation in New Mexico in the year 1943 *Edwin Land* (1901–   ) took a picture of his three-year-old daughter, who subsequently asked why she had to wait so long to see it. What resulted was the development of instant, one-step Polaroid photography.

Albert Einstein

Gerard Swope

Edwin Land

Andre Citröen

Erik Erikson

Marcel Dassault

Sigmund Freud

Charles P. Steinmetz

Jonas Salk

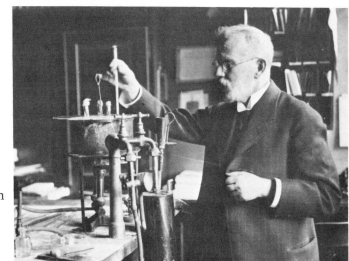

Paul Ehrlich

August von Wassermann

David Sarnoff

Admiral Hyman Rickover

Albert A. Michelson

Emile Berliner

Rosalyn Sussman Yalow

Norbert Wiener

Arthur Kornberg

I. I. Rabi

Selman A. Waksman

Jerome Wiesner

Joshua Lederberg

The son of a remnant merchant, Land entered Harvard as an undergraduate in 1926 but never graduated. Instead, he started manufacturing synthetic polarizers for commercial use by such companies as Eastman Kodak and the American Optical Company.

During World War II, Land's Polaroid Corporation produced and developed improved filters for goggles, gunsights, periscopes, range finders, and aerial cameras. A major project was the development of thermal homing heads containing miniaturized computers attached to the noses of standard thousand-pound bombs. For these and many other contributions Land was awarded the National Medal of Science and the Presidential Medal of Freedom.

Land professes an affinity to the "individual who had freed himself from the way of thinking that is held by friends and associates who may be more intelligent, better educated, better disciplined, but who have not mastered the art of the fresh, clean look at the old knowledge."

The eldest of five children, *David Sarnoff* (1891–1971) arrived in America via steerage in the summer of 1900. Only nine years old, Sarnoff had to peddle papers in the streets to help support his family. Later he left school to become an office boy for the Marconi Wireless Telegraph Company of America.

After taking a special course in electrical engineering at Brooklyn's Pratt Institute, Sarnoff began operating what was then the most powerful radio station in the world atop John Wanamaker's New York store. It was a job Sarnoff never regretted having, for on April 15, 1912, he picked up the message S.S. TITANIC RAN INTO ICEBERG, SINKING FAST. He was the first to receive the SOS signal and report the tragedy to the public.

Three years later, Sarnoff came up with the idea of sending music over the air, which could be picked up by a simple radio. In 1921, as general manager of the recently formed Radio Corporation of America, Sarnoff resubmitted his "music box" idea. Shortly thereafter RCA began to manufacture receiving sets. In 1926, the National Broadcasting Company was launched under Sarnoff's guidance.

Often cited as the father of American television, Sarnoff foresaw the possibilities of this new medium in 1923. Sixteen years later, as president of RCA, Sarnoff made the first public demonstration of television at the New York World's Fair with the words "Now at last we add sight to sound."

An immigrant from Prussia who left school at fourteen, *Emile Berliner* (1851–1929) came to America five years later, in 1870, to seek his fortune.

After working for three years in a Washington, D.C., dry-goods store, Berliner moved to New York, where he sold glue, painted backgrounds for photographs, and gave lessons in German before securing a position in the laboratory of Constantine Fahlberg, who later discovered saccharin.

In his humble capacity as handyman, Berliner learned little more than how to analyze sugar; in the evenings, however, he went to the Cooper Institute at Union Square, where he began studying acoustics and electricity.

In 1876, Alexander Graham Bell invented the telephone. The idea intrigued Berliner. Setting up an electrical laboratory in the small furnished room where he lived, Berliner made the first important discovery leading to the invention of the microphone. He also discovered a method for achieving greater volume and clarity of sound, which assured the success of Bell's invention.

In 1887, Berliner originated a device for the newly invented phonograph that made possible the first disk machine. He called it the Gramophone; it was a milestone in the career of one of the foremost inventors of his time.

Albert Abraham Michelson (1852–1931), the first American to be awarded a Nobel Prize in Physics, was recognized for his work in determining the effects of optical interference on the speed of light. Michelson proved that regardless of the motion of the source or observer, light velocity is constant. This proved to be the foundation of modern experiments with light and is essential to many facets of scientific advancement.

In his mid-sixties, Michelson returned to the navy as a reserve officer and perfected optical range finders and other instruments for use in World War II.

The world's most advanced scientific executive according to Henry Ford, *Gerard Swope* (1872–1957), an early president of the General Electric Company, was born of Jewish parents in St. Louis, Missouri.

When Swope took the reins of General Electric in 1922, its only widely sold product was light bulbs. He diversified the company into consumer items such as radios, vacuum cleaners, refrigerators, and washing machines and led the way to a variety of later products by creating the slogan "More Goods for More People at Less Cost."

There was never a strike at General Electric under Swope's leadership. Before it became customary, 67,000 employees had a profit-sharing plan, unemployment insurance, and cost-of-living wage adjustments.

Swope was a member of the National Labor Board, the Advisory Council on Economic Security , and the Advisory Council on Social Security. He was also chairman of the Coal Arbitration Board, and in 1933 was appointed chairman of the Business Advisory and Planning Council of the U.S. Department of Commerce.

In all his activities, Gerard Swope was described as "a man who was well ahead of other businessmen in vision and sympathy for the welfare of the most humble worker."

When the General Electric Company wanted to engage a consultant with expertise in the theory of alternating current, they hired *Charles Steinmetz* (1865–1923). A brilliant mathematician and electrical engineer who had emigrated from Germany, Steinmetz made his reputation in 1892 on the basis of papers he prepared for the American Institute of Electrical Engineers. He was the first to produce man-made lightning in a laboratory and he developed lightning arresters for protecting transmission lines. His findings are still used in measuring alternating current.

The author of a revolutionary book, *Cybernetics*, published in 1949, *Norbert Wiener* (1894–1964) was considered one of the great mathematicians of our time.

Wiener was born in Columbia, Missouri, the son of Leo and Bertha (Kahn) Wiener. He received a bachelor of arts degree from Tufts College at the age of fifteen and attended Harvard University, where his father was a language professor, for his graduate studies.

His work for the government in World War II included research and the construction of predictors for guided missiles. A study of handling information through radar, servomechanisms, and computers evolved from this war activity and indicated to Wiener that there was a similarity between the human brain and automechanisms. It was an unheard of idea that formed the basis for his book *Cybernetics*.

• IN THE PUBLIC SERVICE •

American Jews have been active in the service of their country since its very beginning. Benjamin Nones, Mordecai Manuel Noah, Isaac Franks, and David Salisbury all served under George Washington. David Franks served as American consul abroad. Haym Salomon contributed substantial amounts to the Revolutionary cause and assisted General Washington in negotiations with European nations.

Presidents Thomas Jefferson and James Madison also had numerous Jewish advisers in whom they placed implicit trust. The Hays family in particular were widely known for their labors on behalf of their fledgling country. John Hays was an administrator of the Indian Territory, and Jacob Hays ultimately became the chief of police of New York City for a period of forty years, gaining worldwide recognition as a "terror" to evildoers.

Philanthropy and community help come naturally to people of Jewish faith because of their long association with problems concerning their own people. This spirit of civic generosity has benefited all groups in our society. Today, we find mayors, governors, and congressmen who come from a tradition of giving honestly and freely of any resource at their command.

Mayor LaGuardia, Governors Lehman and Ribicoff, Senators Javits and Goldwater, and Secretary (of State) Kissinger are dedicated examples of politicians and statesmen of Jewish descent. Supreme Court Justices Cardozo, Frankfurter, and Brandeis set new standards in upholding democratic principles and civil liberties.

Arizona cowboy, Spanish-American war correspondent, American consul in Austria, Ellis Island interpreter, World War I aviator, New York's most memorable mayor—who else could all this be said about but "the Little Flower."

The son of a lapsed Catholic musician from Foggia, Italy, and a Jewish merchant's daughter from Trieste, *Fiorello La-Guardia* (1882–1947) often made campaign speeches in Yiddish. As mayor of New York from 1934 to 1945, LaGuardia earned the respect of even his most vehement critics for building hospitals, schools, airports, highways, and housing developments. Prior to his first election, he warned, "You've nominated me but don't expect any patronage if I'm elected."

No challenge proved too difficult. When a Nazi delegation arrived in New York for the 1939 World's Fair, LaGuardia provided them with an all-Jewish police escort.

During the days of Indian raids and mining booms, Arizona attracted a number of sturdy pioneers, such as *"Big Mike" Goldwater*, a six-foot-three-inch Polish Jewish cap maker who in 1852 went west to make his fortune. In 1872, the Goldwaters opened their first store in the newly founded community of Phoenix. They couldn't make a go of it, but they had better luck in Prescott, the territorial capital.

In 1878, "Big Mike" put up one of the first brick buildings in Prescott. Seven years later he was elected mayor by a large majority.

Mike remained in Arizona for many years with his sons, Morris, Henry, and Baron, the father of Barry Goldwater, the first person of known Jewish background to run for president of the United States.

Belmont Park was named for *August Belmont* (1816–1890), president of the American Jockey Club. Belmont, an ardent art collector, raconteur, consul general for Austria, and minister to the Netherlands, became an influential leader of the Democratic party. He married Caroline Perry, daughter of Commodore Perry.

Born Schönberg, Belmont came to America as a youth,

rented a tiny office on Wall Street and, starting with no funds, established a great banking house. He was a firm supporter of the Union cause and was an adviser to Lincoln and other prominent political leaders.

Supreme Court Justice *Felix Frankfurter* (1882–1965) came to America in 1894 at the age of twelve. Knowing no English, he became obsessed by speech and the written word. At an early age he frequented libraries and reading rooms and attended debates and lectures.

After graduating with honors from Harvard, young Frankfurter was offered a job with a law firm that had never employed a Jewish lawyer. Then came an opportunity to work in Washington with U.S. Attorney General Henry L. Stimson. In 1939, Frankfurter was appointed by President Franklin D. Roosevelt to be a justice of the Supreme Court.

His reverence for American history and tradition can best be summarized in his own words: "Democracy implies respect for the elementary rights of man. . . . A democratic government must practice fairness: and fairness can scarcely be obtained by secret one-sided determination of the facts."

Upon learning that *Louis Dembitz Brandeis* (1856–1941) had been nominated by President Wilson to serve on the Supreme Court, former President Taft called it "one of the deepest wounds I have had as a . . . believer in progressive conservatism." Less than a decade later, Taft, as chief justice, said of Brandeis, "I do not see how we could get along without him."

Much of Taft's initial hostility stemmed from the fact that, to Brandeis's way of thinking, radicalism was not a dirty word. Rather, it was a pledge to seek betterment within the broad lines of existing institutions by refusing to accept as inevitable any evil or immoral practice among businessmen, union leaders, and industrialists.

Ever concerned for the protection of the individual, Brandeis rose to heights of eloquence in his defense of civil liberties. A true democrat, he insisted that "order cannot be secured merely through fear of punishment for its infractions; that it is hazardous to discourage thought, hope and imagination; that fear breeds repression; that repression breeds hate; that hate menaces stable government; that the path of safety lies in the opportunity to discuss freely supposed grievances and proposed remedies; and that the fitting remedy for evil counsels is good ones."

Geographic and religious objections were raised over the appointment of *Benjamin Cardozo* (1870–1938) to the Supreme Court to succeed Oliver Wendell Holmes. There were already two New York justices, Hughes and Stone, and a Jew, Brandeis, on the Supreme Court bench.

When President Hoover disregarded these objections, Idaho Senator William Borah praised him by declaring, "The way to deal with anti-Semitism is not to yield to it."

Using charm and old-world courtesy, Cardozo applied a scholarly detachment and reverence for the law to the complicated problems that came before him in one of the most tumultuous periods in Supreme Court history.

Speaking for all who judge the actions of others, Cardozo wrote, "A judge must be a prophet and historian all in one. [For law is] not only as the past has shaped it in judgments already rendered, but as the future ought to shape it in cases yet to come."

Throughout his life, *Bernard Baruch* (1870–1965) attempted to model his concept of public service after the deeds of his father, a physician, who enlisted in the Confederate army at the beginning of the Civil War.

A Phi Beta Kappa student and an excellent athlete, Baruch's first job was on Wall Street, where he earned three dollars a week. He made his first fortune by the time he was thirty and soon afterward began to give generously to charities.

Baruch was offered the post of secretary of the treasury when Woodrow Wilson assumed the presidency. Baruch refused but became a lifelong admirer of President Wilson, whom he called "the most Christlike man in America."

He became an adviser to Presidents Roosevelt and Truman, as well as John Foster Dulles, James Forrestal, Robert Patterson, and many other leading policy makers. Baruch served as the mobilization czar of World War II, and when he was appointed ambassador to the United Nations' Atomic Energy Committee in 1946, one newspaper editorialized, "We will sleep more comfortably in our beds because clear-eyed Barney Baruch is on guard."

William S. Paley (1901–   ), president and later chairman of the board of CBS, was born in Chicago. His father Samuel and his uncle Jay, immigrants from Russia, were already prospering in the cigar business when young Paley went off to the University of Pennsylvania's Wharton School of Finance to achieve a firmer footing in the business world.

Commercial radio was still in its infancy when Paley made up his mind that this was his field. "My imagination went wild in contemplating the possibilities," he recalled several years after acquiring control of the United Independent Broadcasters in 1928. One year later Paley changed the name of the company to Columbia Broadcasting System. Already, CBS had extended its stations to the Pacific Coast.

At this time Paley introduced noncommercial educational and cultural programs for which the network has become known. Not long afterward, under Paley's direction CBS entered the field of broadcast journalism with such correspondents as Edward R. Murrow, William L. Shirer, and Howard K. Smith.

Between 1941 and 1945 CBS devoted over six thousand hours to war reports and dramatizations. For this Paley was awarded the Legion of Merit and the French Croix de Guerre.

As a pioneer in television, Paley encouraged the development of such programs as *You Are There, Toast of the Town, Studio One,* and the *Arthur Godfrey* programs. Today, after nearly sixty years in broadcasting, Paley remains one of the most highly respected people in his field.

Rear Admiral *Claude C. Bloch* (1878–1967), born in Woodbury, Kentucky, was awarded the Navy Cross during World War I and became Chief of Staff, Battleship Division, in 1921.

After forty years of navy service, Admiral Bloch was made commander-in-chief of the United States Fleet. A model of quiet efficiency, he came through the navy purge following Pearl Harbor without criticism.

Ernest Gruening (1887–1974) attended Hotchkiss and Harvard, receiving first an A.B. and then an M.D. He later gave up medical practice for a political career. He reveals, "I had reached the age of forty-nine and had seen many interesting and beautiful places in Europe and America. But no region ever gave me quite the profound thrill as did Alaska."

In 1939, he was commissioned governor of Alaska.

Alaska was an important military frontier during World War II and was also the source of vital raw materials—tin, chromite, antimony, and nickel. Shortly after forming the Alaskan Territorial Guard in 1942, Governor Gruening enlisted in the war as a commissioned officer.

He believed his greatest accomplishment was the establishment of Alaska as the forty-ninth state.

Felix Frankfurter

Benjamin N. Cardozo

Louis D. Brandeis

Bernard Baruch

Senator Jacob Javits

Senator Abraham Ribicoff

Arthur Burns

Representative Tom Lantos

Senator Rudy Boschwitz

Secretary of Defense Harold Brown

Governor Ernest Gruening

Rebecca Gratz, sister of Benjamin, inspiration for the character of the same name in Sir Walter Scott's *Ivanhoe*

Benjamin Gratz, Organizer and President of the Lexington and Ohio Railroad the second oldest railroad in America

Harvey S. Firestone, Julius Rosenwald, Thomas A. Edison and Thomas Lipton

Mike Goldwater

Representative Barbara Boxer

Senator Edward Zorinsky

Henry Kissinger

Senator Carl Levin

Senator Howard Metzenbaum

Governor Herbert Lehman

Representative Sidney R. Yates

Admiral Claude C. Bloch

August Belmont

Lieutenant General Milton J. Foreman,
First National Commander
of The American Legion

Fiorello LaGuardia with Eleanor Roosevelt

Mayor Diane Feinstein with Pope John Paul II

When *Abe Ribicoff* (1910–   ) was selling newspapers in New Britain, Connecticut, he never dreamed that years later he would take pride in being the only man in the United States Senate who also served as a judge, state legislator, U.S. representative, governor, and presidential cabinet officer.

The son of a Polish-Jewish factory worker who could barely make a living for his family, Ribicoff worked his way through law school before making a mark for himself in Connecticut politics. The first elected official of any stature to predict that John F. Kennedy would become the first Catholic President of the United States, Ribicoff went from serving as governor to becoming Kennedy's secretary of health, education and welfare.

Known by now throughout the country as the governor who initiated a rigorous crackdown on speeding drivers, Ribicoff, as a United States senator, sponsored the country's first Clean Air Act and led in the fight to require the periodic reexamination of all government programs.

Ribicoff once described his long career in politics by saying, "I've been pretty far sighted." Today, there are few who would disagree with one of America's most highly respected public servants.

Arthur F. Burns (1904–   ), only child of Nathan and Sarah Burnseig, entered Columbia University in 1921 on a scholarship. He worked as a seaman, waiter, and house painter. He graduated Phi Beta Kappa, earned a doctorate in economics, and shortly thereafter was appointed a full professor. Named by President Eisenhower in 1953 as his chief economic adviser, he has served in the administration or as a consultant to every succeeding president.

In 1969, President Nixon appointed Burns chairman of the Board of Governors of the Federal Reserve System. In 1971, he told a *Fortune* interviewer, "I think it important

I make my position known. A chairman who sits there until everyone else has made his position known and then votes with the majority—what kind of leadership is that?"

During *Henry Kissinger's* (1923–   ) tenure as secretary of state, Americans felt secure in the knowledge that here was a man, no matter what the problem, who could protect America's interests abroad.

The Kissinger family came from Germany to the United States in 1938; after graduating from high school, Henry Kissinger joined the army. He saw action in the Battle of the Bulge and later served with the Counterintelligence Corps, attaining the rank of captain.

After the war, Kissinger entered Harvard on a scholarship and graduated summa cum laude before obtaining his doctorate.

As a consultant to the army and the Council on Foreign Relations, he attracted the attention of Nelson A. Rockefeller and subsequently served as a consultant to President Eisenhower. In 1969, he became a special assistant to President Nixon for National Security Affairs before being appointed Secretary of State in 1973.

Although our domestic affairs were in disarray, never in history did the United States enjoy as much respect for its international policies than under Henry Kissinger. As President Nixon's secretary of state, he negotiated the first arms limitation agreement with Russia, won a major breakthrough in opening up relations with China, and achieved a remarkable degree of stability in the Middle East.

Harold Brown (1927–   ), secretary of defense under President Jimmy Carter was born in New York, the son of Abraham and Gertrude (Cohen) Brown. His grandparents were Jewish immigrants.

A Phi Beta Kappa scholar, he completed a four-year program in physics and mathematics in half that time at Columbia University and won the Green Memorial Prize for the most outstanding academic record. He later became president of California Institute of Technology, where he was described as "thoughtful, reasonable and brilliant."

Brown is not convinced that advanced technology always produces the most useful weapons under actual field conditions and is inclined toward careful development of weapons systems after exhaustive testing.

He was responsible for a stronger NATO military alliance, with interchangeability of weapons a major factor.

The grandson of an immigrant dry-goods store owner, in 1942 *Howard Metzenbaum* (1917–   ) became the youngest person elected to the Ohio State Legislature up to that time. Already a dedicated advocate of civil rights, in 1943 Metzenbaum introduced a measure that would have banned discrimination by employers and unions on the basis of race, religion, or national origin.

The bill failed; Metzenbaum, however, soon succeeded in pushing through a measure that provided residents of Ohio with consumer protection in credit matters. The Metzenbaum Act subsequently served as a model for the federal Truth-in-Lending Act.

Firmly committed to applying a social conscience to public needs, Metzenbaum expanded his political activities by becoming a candidate for the United States Senate. Though defeated by Robert Taft, Jr., in 1970, he scored a stunning upset over his old opponent six years later.

Soon after taking his seat in the Senate, Metzenbaum denounced deregulation of oil prices, the manufacture of fuel-wasting cars, and the lack of competition in the energy field. Convinced that we must open the way to new sources of fuel, Metzenbaum strongly advocated assisting developing nations to explore for oil and gas. For these and other battles on behalf of the consumer, the Consumer Federation of America has given Metzenbaum consistently high marks.

"I have said publicly that there are too many Democratic senators and Republican senators and not enough United States senators."

This comment typifies the attitude of Nebraska Senator *Edward Zorinsky* (1928–   ) who was reelected to a second six-year term by 67 percent of the vote. Elected mayor of Omaha early in his career, he pushed through major cuts in city spending and continued his approach to spending in the U.S. Senate. There is a framed check for 1.9 million dollars on his wall—money he did *not* spend on staff salaries but returned to the government.

Senator Zorinsky is on the Senate Foreign Relations Committee and the Senate Agricultural Committee and is the three-time winner of the National Federation of Independent Business Award as "Guardian of Small Business" and has also received the Watchdog of the Treasury Award.

Congresswoman *Barbara Boxer* (1940–   ), representing California's Sixth District, is a highly visible new member of Congress who was chosen president of the Democratic New Members Caucus by her peers. She was cited as "a Democratic freshman to watch" by *U.S. News and World Report* and was named one of the "most effective freshmen in the House of Representatives" by the *Congressional Quarterly*.

An articulate advocate for environmental issues, women, senior citizens, small business, education, peace, jobs, and individual rights, Boxer is a strong supporter of "pay as you go" budget proposals. She has introduced a "spare parts" bill, which could save the federal government between $4 and $7 billion per year in military spare parts procurement costs. Her Nuclear Test Ban Challenge resolution has gained national attention as a workable first step toward a nuclear freeze.

As a member of the Government Operations Committee, Congresswoman Boxer serves on the Environment, Energy, and Natural Resources Subcommittee and the Government Operations and Transportation Subcommittee

Congressman *Tom Lantos* (1928–   ) has some rather unusual credentials. He is the first survivor of the Holocaust to be elected to the United States Congress.

A member of the anti-Nazi underground during World War II and a leader of the early postwar anti-Communist student movement in his native Budapest, Congressman Lantos came to the United States in 1947 on a Hillel Foundation scholarship. He received his B.A., M.A., and a Phi Beta Kappa key at the University of Washington, and his Ph.D. at the University of California at Berkeley in the field of international economics.

Lantos worked as a professor of economics, a television analyst, and a business consultant for three decades. His government service includes senior advisory roles in the fields of economics and foreign policy. He is a member of the Committees on Foreign Affairs, Government Operations, and the Aging. He has also served as chairman of the United States Congressional Delegation to the European Parliament/European Common Market.

Who would believe that an immigrant boy, whose family brought him here when he was five years old to escape Hitler's Germany, would attain one of the highest offices in the land? After receiving his law degree from Johns Hopkins University, *Rudy Boschwitz* (1930–   ) served in the Army, practiced law for several years, and then joined his brother's newly formed firm, which acquired an old railroad building in Minneapolis for warehouse purposes.

Senator Boschwitz came into national prominence because of his empathy for small businessmen and farmers. These interests have been carried over into his Senate career. He believes that "a person who has received so much from the American system needs to return it as well," and in his Senate campaign he stressed that "our government needs more representatives from business: men and women who truly understand fiscal responsibility and have a working knowledge of free enterprise."

Eloquent *Dianne Feinstein* (1933–   ), the strikingly handsome mayor of San Francisco, prepared for a governmental career by becoming an expert in criminal justice. "Women often become so divided," she maintains, "they don't zero in on any one thing and their efforts aren't as meaningful. For women to be effective in political life, they've got to have an area of expertise in which they can speak with authority."

When Mayor George Moscone and Board Supervisor Harvey Milk were assassinated on November 27, 1978, Feinstein was elected to complete the mayoral term. She devoted herself to "emotional reconstruction" of San Francisco. "One of the things we need to do is establish priorities in this city," she said, "of what is acceptable behavior and how we generate a community in which diverse elements get along with each other . . . where violence is not condoned. I feel a very great need to heal and bind."

Dianne Feinstein was reelected on a platform of reducing crime, fighting pornography, and curbing high-rise development in downtown San Francisco. Considered a liberal in the beginning of her political career, she has modified her opinions and now stresses fiscal conservatism.

The World of Entertainment
• FILM •

Until recent decades, not all avenues of employment have been open to Jews. One of the few opportunities was within the entertainment industry.

Jewish writers, directors, actors, musicians, dancers, and singers play an important role in molding attitudes and opening avenues both to education and to entertainment through the medium of the cinema. So much of what we think about ourselves and what others assume about us, from Switzerland to Swaziland, emanates from the fertile minds of filmmakers.

Although we have been insulated by two great oceans, we have not become insular, thanks to the power of film to take us to the far reaches of the world. For those who live in even the smallest communities, this giant industry provides a common bond of entertainment and enlightenment.

Theda Bara, Broncho Billy Anderson, and Douglas Fairbanks, Sr., were among the most successful silent film stars. *Fairbanks* (1883–1939) was born Douglas Ulman in Denver, Colorado. In his earliest film he portrayed a likable, unassuming young fellow committed to the belief that America offered boundless opportunities to anyone who dared to live dangerously. In 1920, he reached new heights of popularity when he married Mary Pickford, "America's sweetheart." With *The Mark of Zorro* Fairbanks launched the series of swashbuckler roles with which he has ever since been identified.

Leslie Howard (1893–1943) achieved lasting fame for his portrayal of the genteel Ashley Wilkes in *Gone with the*

Wind. An Englishman by birth, Howard returned to England from the United States at the beginning of World War II to aid in the war effort. Early in 1943 his plane was shot down over Lisbon by the Nazis. On June 12, 1943, a London newspaper reported that "probably no single war casualty has induced such an acute sense of personal loss. Howard . . . was a symbol to the English people. He stood for all that is most deeply rooted in British character."

Cary Grant (1904–   ), another English-born actor of Jewish heritage, is the son of a pants presser. Grant ran away from home at the age of twelve to become a stilt walker. Brought to America in 1920 for an engagement at the New York Hippodrome, Grant stayed on as a Coney Island barker. Several years later, almost by accident, a screen test with a friend's wife initiated a movie career that has balanced romance and comedy in box-office hits spanning nearly half a century.

The son of an Amsterdam, New York, department store clerk, *Kirk Douglas* (1918–   ) (born Issur Danielovitch) left Broadway, after making his debut in 1941 as a singing Western Union messenger in a less than memorable play, to serve in the South Pacific.

Nothing much happened to Douglas's career until his portrayal of an ambitious and unscrupulous prizefighter in the 1949 movie *Champion.* His performance two years later in *Detective Story* catapulted him to success. Since then, Douglas has starred in scores of films in which he has portrayed a mind-boggling variety of personalities.

Shortly after receiving the much-coveted New York Film Critics Award for his riveting interpretation of Vincent Van Gogh, he was asked by John Wayne, "Why did you play that weak, sniveling character?"

"Because I'm an actor," Douglas replied.

Jack Lemmon said of *Judy Holliday* (1923–1965), "She was intelligent and not at all like the dumb blonde she so often depicted . . . She didn't give a damn where the camera was placed, how she was made to look, or about being a star. She just played the scene—acted with, not at. She was also one of the nicest people I've ever met."

Holliday, born Judith Tuvim in New York, had an IQ of 170, but most of her roles in her unfortunately brief career were that of a deadpan, flighty birdbrain.

She turned the role of Billie Dawn opposite Broderick Crawford in *Born Yesterday* into a hilarious masterpiece, winning a best actress Oscar despite the fierce competition of Gloria Swanson in *Sunset Boulevard* and Bette Davis in *All About Eve.*

Miss Holliday's career was cut short by cancer, but she will long be remembered as one of the greatest comic actresses of our time.

"I wasn't driven to acting by any inner compulsion," says *Paul Newman* (1925–   ), who was twenty-six when he left his father's store to enroll in the Yale University School of Drama. "I was running away from the sporting goods business."

One of America's most charismatic actors, Newman has captured the essence of such disparate types as a delinquent-turned-boxer in *Somebody Up There Likes Me,* a pool shark in *The Hustler,* a wisecracking outlaw in *Butch Cassidy and the Sundance Kid,* and a broken-down lawyer in *The Verdict.* Newman is also one of America's most durable sex symbols, with over twenty-eight years in the business and more than forty-five films to his credit.

Nominated and passed over several times for an Academy Award, Newman has been called a victim of the Cary Grant syndrome. He makes everything he does look so easy that everyone assumes he isn't acting. Actually, Newman recalls being terrified by the emotional requirements of acting, which to his way of thinking is "like letting your pants down; you're exposed."

As for the kind of person he is in real life, Newman's friend Gore Vidal calls him a man of "good character [who] would rather not do anything wrong, whether on a moral or an artistic level."

Blond, blue-eyed *Shelley Winters* (1927–   ) is the daughter of a men's clothing designer, Johan Schrift.

From amateur talent contests, to chorus lines, to bit parts, Winters finally landed a minor role in a "B" film, *The Gangster*. She made steady progress in a number of supporting parts and played her first full-length role in 1951. Based on her performance in *A Place in the Sun*, with Elizabeth Taylor and Montgomery Clift, she received the 1952 *Holiday* award as "the woman in the motion picture industry who has done the most in the past year to improve standards and to honestly present American life to the rest of the world."

His role as Sonny Corleone in *The Godfather* brought *James Caan* (1940–   ) an Oscar nomination. James Caan's grandparents emigrated from Nazi Germany, but many members of the family who stayed behind were murdered.

Caan was a pugnacious youngster who learned the hard way to use his fists. Calming down in high school, he became president of his class and captained the baseball and basketball teams.

After what seemed an endless procession of jobs, he enrolled in a New York school of acting. He ultimately received an Emmy nomination in 1971 as best actor in *Brian's Song* viewed by an audience of 60 million.

Douglas Fairbanks, Sr.

Cary Grant

Leslie Howard

Paul Newman

George Segal

Dyan Cannon

Goldie Hawn

Dustin Hoffman

Lauren Bacall

Peter Sellers

Debra Winger

Kirk Douglas

John Houseman

Madeline Kahn

James Caan and Barbra Streisand

Judy Holliday

Joan Collins

Danny Kaye

Luise Rainer and Paul Muni

Edward G. Robinson

Harry Houdini

Jamie Lee Curtis

Paulette Goddard

Tony Curtis

Jill St. John

Melvyn Douglas and Sylvia Sidney

Shelley Winters

Rod Steiger
with Sidney Poitier

Goldie Hawn (1945–   ), whose father played in a society orchestra and whose mother was a wholesale jeweler, was stage struck at Montgomery Blair High School in Silver Spring, Maryland. She studied drama at the American University and took the slow route to stardom dancing in chorus lines from one coast to another.

Goldie Hawn finally hit her stride, accidentally, in "Rowan and Martin's Laugh In" on TV. Producer George Schlatter told *Look*, "We gave her an intro and she blew it, and we broke up. Then we told her to do it again and she blew it again, and then I thought, '*Wait* a minute,' and we started switching cue cards on purpose."

Her engaging personality and sweet naiveté made Goldie much more than a blond stereotype. She acted successfully in *Cactus Flower*, for which she received an Oscar for best supporting actress, *Private Benjamin*, made by her own production company, and many other films.

One of Hollywood's newest stars, *Debra Winger* (1955–   ), was an Oscar nominee for best actress in the film *Terms of Endearment*. Born in Cleveland, Ohio, of Hungarian-Jewish descent, she has received extraordinary reviews in her brief career. Critic Rex Reed (*New York Daily News*) called Winger's portrayal of Paula in *An Officer and a Gentleman* "heartbreaking, three dimensional, seedily lyrical." Janet Maslin (*New York Times*) wrote "[Winger] has such emotional immediacy that she positively glows. Her face is so open and so changeable that she makes Paula's feelings as apparent and as affecting as they can be."

Jack Nicholson, a fellow actor, said of her, "She's a metamorphic actress . . . a genius."

Born Melvyn Hesselberg in Macon, Georgia, *Melvyn Douglas* (1901–1981) was the son of a Russian-born pianist who wanted his only male offspring to become a musician.

Instead, Douglas enlisted in the Canadian Army. His father got him released only to learn two years later that Douglas had joined the United States Army.

After the end of World War I, Douglas did everything from selling pianos, sweaters, and encyclopedias to reading gas meters and running an elevator. Not until 1928 did he make his way to Broadway. Three years later he was brought to Hollywood where he starred in a succession of films with such outstanding leading ladies as Merle Oberon, Constance Bennett, Rosalind Russell, Claudette Colbert, Barbara Stanwyck, and Greta Garbo, who said during the shooting of one of their three movies together, "Douglas knows what a lover should be."

Known as "the man who made Greta Garbo laugh" in *Ninotchka*, Douglas went on to win an Academy Award for best supporting actor in *Hud*. Throughout a long and illustrious film career, he never lost his love for making movies. "You meet as strangers," he remarked, "you begin working together to create something, and this involves trusting one another, searching one another as well as yourself." A rare individual, Douglas continued that search until the day he died.

Born David Daniel Kominski in Brooklyn, New York, *Danny Kaye* (1913–   ) grew up in the household of a struggling tailor from Russia who lacked the money to send his son to college. Realizing that he would not be able to satisfy his childhood dream of becoming a surgeon, Kaye ran away from home to become an entertainer.

After barely getting by with part-time jobs as a soda fountain clerk, an office worker, and an insurance appraiser, Kaye turned to entertaining at private parties as a zany comedian. After performing in summer hotels in the Catskills for a number of years, he was "discovered" by playwright Moss Hart who wrote a part for him in *Lady in the Dark* starring Gertrude Lawrence.

Praised for being "brilliantly funny," Kaye soon became a Hollywood star in such movies as *Up in Arms, The Secret Lives of Walter Mitty,* and *Hans Christian Andersen.* The seventeen films he made in the 1940s and 1950s were largely personal vehicles for what a New York critic described as his "fantastic excursions of clowning."

Looking back on his Hollywood career, Kaye observes: "When I stopped making films, they were getting on to the more explicit films. I gradually moved away from that." Today Kaye is known throughout the world as both a comic and a humanitarian for his work with UNICEF and other worthwhile causes.

Instant stardom and immediate success came to *Lauren Bacall* (1924–   ) in her first movie, *To Have and Have Not,* costarring Humphrey Bogart. The year was 1944. The following year they married and soon became well-known figures on and off the screen.

Born Betty Joan Peske, Lauren Bacall grew up in New York where she attended high school before becoming a fashion model on Seventh Avenue. A picture of her on the cover of *Harper's Bazaar* attracted the attention of a Hollywood talent scout. At the time, the legendary director Howard Hawks was looking for a girl to play opposite Humphrey Bogart. Struck by her superbly photogenic face, Jack Warner of Warner Brothers provided her with the biggest publicity buildup in the studio's history.

After a successful career in Hollywood with such leading men as Charles Boyer, Kirk Douglas, Gary Cooper, and Gregory Peck, Miss Bacall turned her attention to Broadway where she scored major successes in *Cactus Flower* and *Applause,* a musical adaptation of the film *All About Eve* for which she won the much coveted Antoinette Perry Award.

Tall and slender, with an aura of graceful dignity, Lauren Bacall remains one of the most admired women in America today.

Peter Sellers (1925–1980), a relative unknown, entered the entertainment field in a unique manner. Mimicking the voices of two British Broadcasting Corporation stars, he recommended their hiring a rising comedian by the name of Peter Sellers. Astonished by his effrontery but impressed by the masquerade, he was hired for a radio show and went on from there to the *Goon Show* which literally shattered every British pretension.

Brown haired, brown eyed, five feet ten inches tall, Sellers was a Jewish political liberal who was absolutely inactive in politics, but was fascinated by judo, cricket, complicated stereo equipment, musical instruments, automobiles, and gadgets of all kinds.

Described as a man with a thousand voices, Sellers starred as a buffoonish French detective in several comedies where his amazing ear for accents revealed uncanny mimicry. In *I'm All Right, Jack,* he portrayed a pompous shop steward with a cockney accent. Bosley Crowther said of his performance, "He is all efficiency, righteous indignation, monstrous arrogance and blank ineptitude—he is also sidesplittingly funny, as funny as a true stuffed shirt can be."

Dyan Cannon (1937–   ) still refers to Cary Grant as "my husband" even though they were divorced years ago. Perhaps it has something to do with the product of that marriage, Jennifer Grant, Dyan's only child as well as Cary's only offspring after a quintet of marriages.

The daughter of a Jewish mother and Dutch Protestant father, Dyan was raised as a Jew in Seattle while her brother, David, a jazz musician, took on the religion of their father. A former Miss Seattle, Dyan was "discovered" in a Los

Angeles restaurant by a movie producer who promptly changed her name from Samille Diane "Frosty" Friesen to an "explosive" new name. Her breakthrough came in 1969 with the movie *Bob & Carol & Ted & Alice*. Since then she has starred in numerous films highlighting her gift for comedy, often punctuated by an enormous wild laugh that fills the room.

Dyan lives in Malibu, on the beach where she wears "jeans and T-shirts and when I come out in the world, I say, 'Oh, is *that* what's going on?' because I don't read newspapers, I don't have a TV." A sign of her seriousness is a photograph of Einstein on the wall of her Malibu home. "Isn't he cute?" she says. "Now there's a sexy man!"

Growing up in a middle-class WASP neighborhood in Kansas City, in a strict Orthodox Jewish household, *Ed Asner* (1929–   ) was elected all-city tackle while he was on the Wyandotte High School football team.

Involved in a number of drama projects at the University of Chicago, he dropped out after several years and worked as an automobile mechanic, a molder in a steel mill, finally doing a stint in the army. Discharged in Chicago, Asner joined a Chicago repertory theatre where he gained considerable experience.

Asner's star began to rise when he moved to Los Angeles. His role of a police chief in a television movie aroused the interest of Mary Tyler Moore's husband who was about to launch a new show—he was given the role of Lou Grant, a tough, dominating boss with a sentimental soft spot. Since then, the depth of his performances has earned him many superlative critical comments, five Emmy awards and recognition as one of the nation's most civic-minded actors, participating in Common Cause, the National Committee for an Effective Congress, and Americans for Democratic Action.

Dr. Peshkowsky fled with his family from Nazi Germany to New York in the late 1930s where he assumed the name of Nichols and set up a medical practice.

His son, *Mike Nichols* (1931–   ), studied at "very chic, very progesssive schools, where we were taught French from playing cards and were served something every hour—second breakfast, mid-morning snack, hearty lunch, early afternoon cookies."

Giving up his formal education after two years at the University of Chicago, Nichols, six feet tall, blond and blue-eyed, joined a night club group which included Elaine May. With her, he improvised comedy sketches which established a format for future performances. Brilliant satirists, Walter Kerr said of them, "There is malice, you see, behind the making with the jokes—Truth snakes in and rears its venomous head, looking sparkling and ugly at the very same time, without for a moment interrupting the rolling laughter."

An outstanding artist, actor, producer, and director with many hits to his credit, Mike Nichols' direction of the 1985 hit play *Hurlyburly* has brought him even more critical acclaim.

• TELEVISION •

Just a little more than a generation ago television began revolutionizing our lives to an even greater degree than films. It has subtly changed our dependence on the printed word, catapulted athletic events into a world of commercialism, given us instantaneous coverage of fast-breaking news, and led to restructuring our most basic institution, the family unit.

Whatever the consequences, television's power to influence our lives is incalculable. Its scope is limitless, encompassing everything from the pronouncements of presidential candidates to the distractions of low comedy.

Many viewers complain about the emphasis placed on crime and violence, but television has also contributed attractive role models for teenagers, such as "the Fonz," the flip, audacious, leather-jacketed, outrageously brash character in "Happy Days," as portrayed by Henry Winkler, the son of German Jews who survived the Holocaust; Lorne Greene as Ponderosa patrician Ben Cartwright in "Bonanza"; or Charles Ingalls, pioneer family man in "Little House on the Prairie" as played by Michael Landon.

The series "Star Trek," a science-fiction fantasy, has become a national institution supporting hundreds of fan clubs, nearly five hundred fan publications, and annual conventions attracting thousands of faithful enthusiasts. TV's exploration of space by two Jewish actors, *William Shatner* (1931–   ) and *Leonard Nimoy* (1931–   ), has been compared to the uncharted travels of Christopher Columbus, who, some believe, was Jewish.

"There's only one thing worse than a man who doesn't have strong likes and dislikes and that's a man who has strong likes and dislikes without the courage to voice them."

That is the opinion of *Tony Randall* (1910–   ), the crazy-clean, cigar-hating, elegant Felix of TV's "The Odd Couple." Born in Tulsa, Oklahoma, the son of an antique dealer, Randall was always intrigued with acting. Early in his career he depended on radio work. After serving four years in the army, Randall played a number of supporting roles on Broadway before achieving broad recognition in a number of Rock Hudson/Doris Day comedies. As a jealous suitor in *Pillow Talk,* one critic called Randall "one of the funniest young men in movies today," before adding that he deserved to be in a better picture.

In the role of Harvey Weskit in the TV series "Mr. Peepers," he became an international star. It led to his popular role in "The Odd Couple." This talented actor is also a commentator on performances of the Metropolitan Opera and has served as a music and art critic.

"This script is ridiculous. We talk all through the show about this giant guy with superhuman strength who breaks people's necks with his fingers, and then in the climax, a fifty-four-year-old character like me gives him one crack on the head and takes him out. I'm supposed to be a doctor, right? What kind of a doctor goes around hitting people anyway?" bellows *Jack Klugman* (1922–   ) about a scene in TV's "Quincy."

Klugman wanted to do a "doctor" series as a dramatic "thank you" to a surgeon who saved his acting career by performing a successful and delicate cancer operation on his larnyx.

Klugman's five-year stretch as Oscar in "The Odd Couple" catapulted him to fame and fortune.

"Not only an excellent actress, but one of the most professional I have ever worked with. She's never late. She does not have a temper. She's given an enormous amount to other actors. She's straight and gutsy," writes Lynn Loring describing Joan Collins in "Dynasty."

Cast as Blake Carrington's cold-blooded ex-wife, Alexis, in this top-rated TV series, *Joan Collins* (1936–   ) admits that it is the best vehicle of her career.

Glamorous, sultry Collins was born in England of Dutch and French ancestry. Her Jewish father, a theatrical agent, brought guests home, and Joan, enamored of these entertainers, fantasized that one day she would be a famous actress. Her dream has come true.

Born Eugene Maurice Orowitz in Forest Hills, New York, *Michael Landon* (1937–   ) first earned recognition as a javelin thrower (he achieved a national high school record in the early fifties). After suffering injuries to his arm, Landon dropped out of college and worked as a process server, blanket salesman, car washer, and factory hand before deciding to sign up for classes at the Warner Brothers acting school. The professional name he chose came from the Los Angeles telephone book.

Landon's rugged good looks won him a number of small roles on television as well as the title role in *I Was a Teenage Werewolf*, a horror movie that still haunts Landon on late-night TV.

In 1959, Landon was asked to read for the part of Little Joe Cartwright, the headstrong youngest son in "Bonanza." Landon played the role of Little Joe for fourteen years. Seen by an estimated 400 million viewers, "Bonanza" became one of the most popular television shows ever produced.

In 1964, Landon won the Silver Spurs Award as "the most popular TV western star" in America. Next came an equally successful series, "Little House on the Prairie," with Landon starring as Charles Ingalls, a hard working, upright pioneer father.

Peter Falk (1927–) dreamed of being on the stage but felt that "ordinary people don't become actors." However, as *Time* magazine quoted him, "I stopped by a theater in New Haven and followed Roddy McDowall, Estelle Winwood and Maria Diva to lunch just to hear what they'd talk about. The conversation was absolutely banal and here I thought they were all geniuses."

At twenty-eight, he left Ossining, New York, where his parents ran a small clothing store, and moved to New York City. He played on Broadway and then moved to Hollywood, where he starred in *Murder, Inc., Pocketful of Miracles, It's a Mad, Mad, Mad, Mad World, The Great Race,* and many more movies.

Television turned out to be the perfect medium for Falk. Perhaps the role that suited him best was "Columbo." John Cassavetes said of him, "He's deep. He's gentle. He's two thousand years old. He's somebody everybody falls in love with."

Nebraska-born *David (Meyer) Janssen* (1930–1981) made his acting debut at the age of three on a vaudeville stage with his mother, a former Ziegfeld show girl and Miss America runner-up. A decade or so later he played Johnny Weissmuller's younger brother in a long-forgotten Paramount picture.

Limited to minor roles in the movies, Janssen jumped at the chance to play the title role in "Richard Diamond, Private Detective" on television. The year was 1957. The show provided a major boost to Janssen's career.

Returning to the movies, Janssen appeared in a string of hit-and-run adventures in which his talents were largely wasted. Not until 1962 did opportunity knock again in the form of a call from a TV producer; he asked Janssen to read for the part of a rootless man who, through no fault of his own, is pursued for a crime he never committed. The result was "The Fugitive."

A darkly handsome man with a manner that reflected a tough, terse decency, Janssen seemed made for the role. Though one critic was quick to point out that Janssen "commands the narrowest gamut of facial expressions of any actor since the late Alan Ladd," Janssen was nonetheless voted favorite male performer in a 1964 reader poll taken by *TV Guide*.

The only child of a Bucharest grain merchant, *John Houseman* (1902–   ) (born Jacques Hausemann) moved to New York City in 1924 to accept a job with the Continental Grain Corporation. When the stock market collapsed five years later, Houseman decided to become a theatrical producer and director, even though he had no prior training or experience in the field.

His first success came as a Broadway director on an all-black production of the Gertrude Stein–Virgil Thomson opera *Four Saints in Three Acts*. This was followed by a memorable collaboration with Orson Welles in such Mercury Theatre productions as a modern-dress version of *Julius Caesar* and a radio drama of H. G. Wells's *The War of the Worlds*, which panicked some listeners into believing that America had been invaded by Martians.

In the forties and fifties, Houseman turned his attention to Hollywood, where he soon earned a reputation for doing projects no one else could. During this period he produced a score of critically acclaimed motion pictures, including *Executive Suite, Julius Caesar*, and *Lust for Life*.

Houseman's own acting career, which began with his portrayal of an irascible professor in the film *Paper Chase* (he repeated the role in the TV series of the same name), has included everything from playing Winston Churchill in

"Meeting at Potsdam" to making television commercials for a leading investment counseling firm.

George Burns (1896–   ) was born Nathan Birnbaum on New York's Lower East Side. Together with Gracie Allen, a delightful young Irish-American actress, they worked their way up to the top of the entertainment field. They were married in 1926 and continued as a team in vaudeville, movies, radio, and TV until Gracie retired in 1958. When she died in 1964, he went on performing, frequently recalling experiences with Gracie. He visits her grave twice a month. "I tell her everything I'm doing. I know she'll never come back," he remarks, "but to me she really isn't gone."

"Ladies and Gentlemen, this is *Jack Benny* (1894–1974) talking. There will be a slight pause while you say, 'Who cares?' " That was in 1932.

Benny, born Benjamin Kubelsky in Waukegan, Illinois, was a violinist turned stand-up comedian. He promoted a "miser" image, but was far from it in real life. Eddie Anderson, who played the part of his chauffeur, Rochester, was the highest-paid black actor in radio in the early 1940s. One of Benny's best-known jokes involved a holdup man who stopped him and said, "Your money or your life!" A lengthy pause followed. The robber screamed, "Look, bud, you heard me. Your money or your life!" Benny replied petulantly, "I'm thinking, I'm thinking."

At Benny's funeral, Bob Hope observed, "Jack Benny had that rare magic—that indefinable something called genius. . . . For a man who was the undisputed master of comedy, *this* was the only time Jack's timing was wrong. He left us too soon."

William Shatner

Jack Klugman   Tony Randall

Hal Linden

Henry Winkler

Peter Falk

William S. Paley

Ed Asner

Lorne Greene

George Burns
with Gracie Allen

Werner Klemperer

David Janssen

Jack Benny

Michael Landon

Gene Barry

Bonnie Franklin

Linda Lavin

Paul Michael Glaser

Ted Koppel

Howard Cosell

Barbara Walters

Mike Wallace

Born in Winston-Salem, North Carolina, *Howard Cosell* (1920–   ) (Cohen) was admitted to the bar at the age of twenty-nine and opened a law office in Manhattan after attaining the rank of major in World War II.

An American Broadcasting Company program manager asked Cosell in 1953 if he would like to host a radio show in which youngsters interviewed professional baseball players. Cosell accepted and, after three years, gave up his legal practice and signed a full-time contract with ABC.

Over the years, Cosell has refused to read prepared scripts or use teleprompters, insisting rather on ad-libbing. His direct approach has alienated some sport fans, but most appreciate his attempts to ascertain the truth.

With the sharpest tongue of all sports announcers, Howard Cosell has forthrightly displayed his resentment of racism in all forms.

The child of refugees who escaped Hitler's Germany just before the outbreak of World War II, *Edward James Koppel* (1940–   ) was born in England. In 1953, the Koppels migrated to New York City. After graduating from Stanford University in 1962, Koppel became a news commentator for ABC radio. Impressed by his talent for clarifying issues, ABC News officials transferred him to Vietnam in 1967. Five years later he was assigned to accompany President Nixon on his historic trip to China.

His present position as the guiding light of ABC News "Nightline" began in 1979. Millions of viewers admire Koppel's direct approach on this thinking man's news series, as well as his riveting spontaneity. "I do these shows to educate myself as much as anyone else," Koppel observes. "Our standard is, if it interests those of us who produce the show, then it will interest [others]."

No stranger to show business herself, *Barbara Walters* (1931–   ) is the daughter of Lou Walters, owner of New York's Latin Quarter and many other nightclubs.

A graduate of Sarah Lawrence College, Walters had hoped to become an actress before starting her career in broadcasting as an assistant to the publicity director of NBC, where she became adept in all phases of writing and producing TV programs. Fame came later as anchorwoman on the NBC "Today Show."

"She asks some of the toughest questions in television journalism—dumdum bullets swaddled in angora," observed *Newsweek* about her uncanny ability to get her guests to divulge their most well-kept secrets. In one interview Truman Capote confessed to her, "It's my essentially tragic nature that makes me do the frivolous things I do."

Poised, attractive, intelligent, Barbara Walters is admired today by millions of viewers as *not* just another pretty face.

Mike Wallace (1918–   ), the son of Russian immigrants, has had a stunning impact on television audiences for over thirty years. "60 Minutes," a tough, aggressive, bitingly candid magazine-format show, has developed into a TV institution. A consummate showman who has never shied away from controversy, Wallace has sought out such personalities as the Grand Wizard of the Ku Klux Klan, racketeer Mickey Cohen, Communist party leader Earl Browder, former attorney general John Mitchell, black activist Eldridge Cleaver, and the American soldiers involved in the My Lai massacre in Vietnam.

A superb interrogator, he opens his interviews softly because, he explains, "You want to put a man at ease. You waste a few, like a baseball pitcher."

Wallace has used his unique talents to uncover such scandals as Medicaid fraud and kickbacks from dishonest medical laboratories; he has investigated heroin rings, draft evasion, and child beating. In his own words, "We probe personality close up, look at sex head on, hate cats if necessary, and try to knock the starch out of a couple of stuffed shirts."

• MUSIC •

Jewish contributions to music are astounding—from Meyerbeer, Offenbach, and Mendelssohn in Europe to Berlin, Gershwin, and Bernstein in the United States.

Tapping our native roots—minstrels, ragtime, jazz, rhythm and blues, and folk-rock—great composers, conductors, and vocal artists have played a major role in putting American music on the map. "Rhapsody in Blue" released jazz from Tin Pan Alley and made *George Gershwin* (1898–1937) famous. Gershwin's formidable talents led to worldwide recognition of his music, particularly his folk opera, *Porgy and Bess*.

Before his untimely death at the age of thirty-nine, he wrote the score for and orchestrated such musical comedies as *Girl Crazy, Of Thee I Sing,* and *Funny Face.* Two films based on his music and his life, were produced: respectively, *An American in Paris* and *Rhapsody in Blue.*

Though born into a Jewish family, *Jerome Kern* (1885–1945) frequently walked miles to listen to choir practice at an Episcopal church, where the harmonics made a deep impression on the youthful musician. Inspired to compose his own songs, within the space of seven years he created nine musicals, among them *Sally, Sunny,* and *Showboat.*

Author Edna Ferber, describing her initial reaction to Kern's playing of "Ol' Man River," raved, "The music mounted, mounted, and I give you my word my hair stood on end, tears came to my eyes and I breathed like a heroine in a melodrama. This was great music. This was music that would outlast Jerome Kern's day and mine. I have never heard it since without an emotional surge."

Equally noteworthy are *Richard Rodgers* (1902–1979) and *Oscar Hammerstein* (1895–1960), whose *Oklahoma!* marked the beginning of a new operetta form, culminating in such major works as *South Pacific* and *The King and I*. Discarding every music hall cliché, they developed a fresh theatrical structure. With a touch of idealism our basic values were woven into a cultural form that helped to improve the world's vision of America.

While Rodgers and Hammerstein were enthralling audiences on Broadway, *Dinah Shore* (1921–   ), born Fanny Rose Shore in Winchester, Tennessee, was collecting Emmies, gold records, and a string of Motion Picture Daily Poll "firsts" as the best female vocalist on radio, TV, and records.

Beverly Sills (1929–   ), a leading American soprano, has an enormous warmth and range. "If I were recommending the wonders of New York City to a tourist," music critic Winthrop Sargent said of Sills while she was at the height of her career, "I should place Beverly Sills as 'Manon'at the top of the list—way ahead of such things as the Statue of Liberty and the Empire State Building." She is now director of the New York City Opera.

"Reaching out to people with music is one of the most deeply moving experiences you can have," declared *Leonard Bernstein* (1918–   ), and if you have had the good fortune to see *West Side Story*, you will agree that he, indeed, reaches out to us.

This masterful musician has no equal in communicating his enthusiasm and diverse skills through his play scores, his classical compositions, and his dynamic conducting. Bernstein has been the recipient of Emmy Awards for his TV concerts for young audiences, New York Music Critics

Circle Awards, Academy Award nominations, and practically every other honor it is possible to receive in his field.

Eddy Duchin (1909–1951) was the "one in a million" pianist with perfect pitch. It enabled him to extemporize, orchestrate novel arrangements, and become one of America's most noted musicians.

He led his own band until the outbreak of World War II when, as the son of German Jewish immigrants, he felt it his duty to volunteer for service in the navy—refusing the privilege offered to most celebrities of taking a desk job.

Assigned to the Third Fleet, Duchin was honorably discharged as a lieutenant commander and presented with a citation for meritorious service just before he died at the age of forty-one.

Copenhagen-born *Victor Borge* (1909–   ) made the Nazis the butt of some of his drollest remarks. On the signing of a nonaggression pact between Denmark and Germany shortly before the outbreak of World War II, Borge quipped, "Now the good German citizens can sleep peacefully in their beds, secure from the threat of Danish aggression."

Soon after the Germans invaded Denmark in 1940, Borge managed to escape to America in the hold of an overcrowded ship. In a matter of a few years he was commanding the attention of a nationwide audience with his inimitable wit and style. When a critic wrote, "Borge is a good pianist but he's no Horowitz," Borge replied, "That should come as a relief to the parents of Horowitz."

Music and the light touch remain Borge's trademarks, as millions have learned during a career spanning over sixty years.

In the sixties and seventies, such vocalists as *Bob Dylan* (1941–   ) and *Billy Joel* (1949–   ) ignited an entire generation with their folk-rock songs. Dylan, born Bob Zimmerman, has been praised for expressing genuine concern about people in his songs, and Billy Joel has achieved worldwide recognition for ballads that are new, tough, brash.

The son of Austrian Jewish parents whose family name is derived from the German word for "fiddler," *Arthur Fiedler* (1894–1979) came from a long line of musicians, primarily violinists.

He was born in the Back Bay section of Boston and, after completing three years at the prestigious Boston Latin School, traveled to Europe with his father, a violinist with the Boston Symphony Orchestra. Soon afterward, young Fiedler was accepted into Berlin's exclusive Royal Academy of Music.

Following in his father's footsteps, Fiedler returned to America to become a violinist for the Boston Symphony Orchestra. Later, he switched to the viola, and then to other instruments—piano, organ, celesta, percussion. "I did everything except sweep the floors," Fiedler recalled years later.

In 1927 he started a campaign to finance free open-air concerts in the heart of Boston, a radical idea at the time. Since 1929 the Esplanade concerts have been an annual event. In the following year, Fiedler became the leader of the Boston Pops, a position he held for half a century. An astute showman, Fiedler made the Pops the first large orchestra in the country to play everything from classical music to rock 'n roll.

As indigenous to Boston as the cod and the Cabots, Fiedler was also one of the most prominent musical personalities in the country, with total sales of 50 million discs as proof of his success in creating a bridge between popular and classical music.

• ART •

In the past, two factors conspired to prevent Jews from becoming artists: religious prohibition against making graven images and the inability of an impoverished and persecuted people to sustain anything but minimal art forms. Even in this century, Chaim Soutine had to leave Russia because as an artist he had brought shame upon his family.

America provided the freedom for artists to fulfill themselves. A veritable explosion resulted. George Segal, Mark Rothko, Helen Frankenthaler, Adolph Gottlieb, Franz Kline, Roy Lichtenstein, Jim Dine, Abraham Ratner, and Ben Shahn, have all experimented in a variety of brilliant art forms.

Mark Rothko (1901–1970), a member of the "New York school," was a pioneer abstract painter who relied purely on the use of color to establish poetic and sensuous moods.

Ben Shahn (1898–1969) was a political realist who used his subject matter as a statement to point out inequities in our social system.

Roy Lichtenstein (1923–   ) grew out of the pop art movement. Using comics as a point of departure, he utilizes mundane, everyday objects to emphasize the crass commercialism of his world.

George Segal (1924–   ) makes replicas of his friends by encasing them in plaster. The resulting figures, after his reshaping, assume an almost ghostly presence. Each sculpture appears to have its own personality—but all are indifferent, turning away, stressing man's basic loneliness.

Renowned worldwide, with numerous books and countless articles written about her and even a New York City plaza named in her honor, *Louise Nevelson* (1900–   ) has come a long way since her birth in Kiev, Russia.

Mr. and Mrs. Irving Berlin with President Eisenhower

Dinah Shore

Beverly Sills

Bob Dylan

Billy Joel

Barry Manilow

Arthur Fiedler

Rise Stevens

George Gershwin

Scene from *Porgy and Bess*

Scene from *Show Boat*

Jerome Kern

Richard Rodgers and
Oscar Hammerstein, II

Scene from
Oklahoma

Scene from
South Pacific

Leonard Bernstein

Victor Borge

Eddie Duchin

Vladimir Horowitz

Marc Chagall

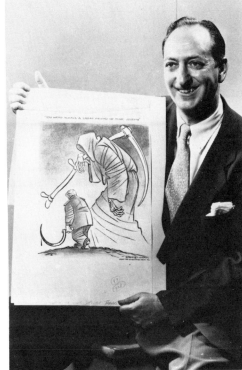

Herbert L. Block

Al Capp

Louise Nevelson

Amedeo Modigliani

Margaret Bourke-White

Camille Pissarro

Chartres Cathedral
by Chaim Soutine

Her family, the Berliawskys, emigrated to Rockland, a small town in Maine, where she was honored recently as a celebrity, a far cry from the anti-Semitism she experienced as a young girl.

Nevelson's unique, exciting style was developed using prosaic wooden odds and ends. "One reason for my use of 'found' materials," she explains, "is that I could never afford much else. But now that I'm economically free . . . there's nothing I can't use: plastic, plexiglass, metal. I've lived all this time just for those new materials."

Seeking inspiration everywhere, this extraordinary woman has traveled to Germany, Austria, Mexico, Central America, and Africa. One of her masterpieces is a quiet, all white chapel designed for meditation in the Citicorp Building in New York. It was commissioned by St. Peter's Church.

Objecting to his "wasting time" as a poet and dancer, *Marc Chagall* (1887–1985) was indentured to a Vitebsk photographer by his parents. Chagall resented destroying the character in customers' faces by touching up their wrinkles and, at the earliest opportunity, left Russia for Paris to study art. Years elapsed before he received recognition for his mystical, imaginative paintings. For a time, he was so poor that he used his bed sheets, shirts, and pajamas for canvases.

Chagall attained fame and fortune with his fanciful representations of lovers hovering in the air, cows in the heavens, and fiddlers on rooftops.

Chagall said of his work, "[It] is a wild art, a blazing quicksilver, a blue soul flashing on canvas."

Artists receive much of their inspiration from those who have preceded them. Today's artists owe a great debt to Modigliani, Soutine, and Pissarro.

Mary Cassatt said of *Camille Pissarro* (1830–1903), "He could have taught a stone to draw."

The father of Impressionism, Camille Pissarro was born in the Virgin Islands, the son of a Jewish father and a Creole mother. He pleaded with his parents for art instruction, but was refused. Eventually he traveled to Paris, where he became the mentor of fellow artists Manet, Monet, Renoir, Gauguin, Seurat, and Sisley.

Using vibrations of light as a dominant theme and abandoning exact contour and precise detail, the Impressionists were at first looked upon much as pop artists were more recently. In fact, Napoleon III had to intervene on behalf of the Impressionist group in order to have their paintings exhibited in an important Parisian salon showing.

Pissarro, Monet, Sisley fled Paris for England during the Franco-Prussian War. When Pissarro returned, he found his residence ransacked and nearly a thousand of his paintings mutilated.

After becoming an invalid in mid-career, Pissarro painted subtle, poetic versions of rainy Paris boulevards from his second-story apartment window; these were later considered to be among his richest, most powerful works.

Passionate, romantic, proud, handsome, *Amedeo Modigliani* (1884–1920) never found recognition or buyers for his work. The son of Italian Orthodox Jews, during his brief life Modigliani lived for his art, above all else. Unable to compromise, refusing to cheapen himself or his painting, Modigliani was a great artist who, despite a bitter personal life, managed to leave an enduring artistic legacy.

No one has better described the genius of the artist than Modigliani's biographer, Pierre Sichel: "Great artists are more fortunate than great kings, statesmen, generals, and dictators in that they reverse Shakespeare's lines about the evil men do living after them and the good being oft interred with their bones. They leave neither new countries nor divided ones, neither civilizations in bondage nor hopes and opportunities denied, nor a people crushed or murdered. They leave in their paintings, sculptures, symphonies and books an imperishable legacy. More than most, artists truly 'make good the honor of being man.' "

The tenth child of a destitute tailor whose family lived in a one-room hovel in a Russian village near Minsk, *Chaim Soutine* (1894–1943), by drawing pictures, broke an ancient religious law forbidding portraiture of a human figure. Sent off at the age of sixteen, Soutine eventually found his way to Paris.

Painting was his entire world; he knew no other. Perpetually poor, Soutine experienced a great reversal when Dr. Albert Barnes, the Argyrol king, bought out his complete inventory of paintings in Paris in 1923. With the proceeds Soutine went down the narrow stairway leading from his studio to the street, hailed a taxi (a luxury he could never afford before), and said, "Take me to the Riviera!"

· THE WRITTEN WORD ·

Great writers and chroniclers of our time—Theodore White, Saul Bellow, Lillian Hellman, Dorothy Parker, William Safire, Arthur Miller, Joseph Heller—have enormously influenced the way we read, write, and hear our language. There is a refreshing element of inconsistency in their views, reflecting divergent attitudes that encompass the length and breadth of this country.

"Today the novelist thinks too much of immortality. . . . I kicked over the traces, wrote catch-as-catch-can, picaresque. I took my chance." It was the right approach for *Saul Bellow* (1915–   ), who in 1976 won the Nobel Prize for literature.

Bellow, whose father, Abraham, was a small retailer, achieved fame in his thirties with the publication of his third novel, *The Adventures of Augie March,* which won him the first of three National Book Awards plus a Pulitzer Prize and sold over a million copies in paperback.

Bellow's heroes are men caught in the middle of spiritual crises yet rejecting both easy optimism and instant despair in their search for a moral justification to life suited to their temperaments and personalities.

Bellow believes that the creation of art has a certain kinship with religion: "I feel that art has something to do with the achievement of stillness in the midst of chaos. A stillness which characterizes prayer, too, and the eye of the storm."

America's most successful woman playwright, *Lillian Hellman* (1905–1984) was born in New Orleans, the daughter of a struggling shoe salesman. Her sharp, incisive depictions of the South were gleaned from her experience growing up there.

When Herman Shumlin agreed to produce *The Children's Hour*, Hellman had fifty dollars to her name. Although highly controversial for its time, the play ran long enough on Broadway to make Hellman $125,000 richer.

Hellman was a strong-willed moralist who insisted that the theater is useless unless it raises social consciousness. *The Little Foxes*, whose title comes from the Scriptures and was suggested by Dorothy Parker, is an updated morality tale of rapacious people intent on destroying anyone in their path.

In *Watch on the Rhine*, which premiered in New York in 1941, Hellman expressed contempt for the Nazis by showing an American family with split loyalties suddenly awakening to the dangers threatening their liberties.

A courageous individualist, Lillian Hellman insisted on her right as a writer "to say that greed is bad or persecution is worse . . . without being afraid that I will be called names or end in a prison camp or be forbidden to walk down the street at night."

Journalist, historian, chronicler of American presidential campaigns—*Theodore H. White* (1915–   ), in addition to his best-selling *The Making of the President* books, has written two novels, one play, dozens of magazine articles, and several TV documentaries.

A reporter for well over forty years, White is often praised for the grace and ease of his style, his flair for narration, and his general professional competence. "I'm flattered that people call me a historian," White confides, "but I'm just the man who happens to be around when things happen, and I like to tell stories about them." Some of these stories White tells in Yiddish or Hebrew.

One of four children of a struggling lawyer, White entered

Harvard on a newsboy's scholarship and graduated summa cum laude. The recipient of a traveling fellowship, White ended up in China, where he reported for the *Boston Globe* on the bombing of Peking. "Once I had seen that," White explained years later, "I knew I wasn't going home to be a professor."

After serving as chief of *Time*'s China bureau, White returned to the United States before moving to Paris, where he reported on Europe's remarkable postwar recovery. Not until 1956 did he begin reporting on presidential elections. Three years later the idea for *The Making of the President 1960* occurred. Bringing to his task "the eye of the novelist and the perceptions of the reporter," White soon developed into America's preeminent political journalist—a position he has maintained for over twenty years.

A ward of at least six different foster homes, *Art Buchwald* (1925–   ) dropped out of school at the age of sixteen and joined the Marine Corps during World War II.

In 1948, he started his career as a reporter reviewing films for the Paris edition of the *New York Herald Tribune* at a salary of twenty-seven dollars a week. His column is now featured in nearly five hundred newspapers.

A humorist who finds nothing sacred in Washington or anywhere else, Buchwald, also a highly esteemed public speaker, has appeared as a guest on numerous television shows and has written over twenty books.

This masterful satirist married Ann McGarry, whom he met in Paris. "We both had the same black market money changer," he says. About their three adopted children Buchwald exclaims dourly, "They'd better come up with a couple of column ideas each week or out they go." One thing he doesn't require of them is physical activity. He claims that exercise is "dangerous" and prefers a "horizontal" position at all times.

Saul Bellow with King Carl Gustaf
of Sweden

Lillian Hellman

Dorothy Parker

Arthur Miller

Joseph Heller

Mike Nichols

Katherine Graham

Tom Stoppard

Gloria Steinem

Joyce Brothers

William Safire

Joseph Pulitzer

Theodore H. White

Abigail Van Buren

Ann Landers

Art Buchwald

Edwin Newman

With satirical wit, tiny, demure *Dorothy Parker* (1893–1967) (born Dorothy Rothschild) exposed the superficial banalities and cloying sentimentalism of her day in scores of articles, movies, and plays. The first woman to be accepted as an equal by the wits of the Algonquin "Round Table"—Alexander Woollcott, Robert Benchley, George S. Kaufman, Harold Ross, among others—she was the mistress of the fast barb that deflated all pretensions.

"Don't worry about Alan," Parker commented about the husband she had recently divorced, "he will always land on somebody's feet." Describing an acquaintance with a lively love life, she quipped, "You know, that woman speaks eighteen languages, and she can't say no in any of them."

In her memoirs, Lillian Hellman warmly remembers her longtime friend: "I enjoyed her more than I have enjoyed any other woman . . . her view of people was original and sharp, her overelaborate manners made her a pleasure to live with. She liked books and was generous about writers, and the wit, of course, was so wonderful that neither age nor illness ever dried up the spring from which it came fresh each day."

Ann Landers and *Abigail Van Buren* (1918–   ), "the Friedman twins," were adorable look-alikes with coal-black hair and spectacular blue eyes. As little girls, they wore their hair short, with bangs, giving them the look of two street extras in *The Mikado*. They were precocious, peppy, pretty—and always dressed alike.

Born in Sioux City, Iowa, the twins were inseparable until their identical careers, answering letters from the lovelorn, created a fierce competitive situation.

A United Press poll named Ann Landers one of the ten most important women in the United States. Her readership is so extensive that she has employed up to thirteen secretaries to answer her mail.

Abigail Van Buren's "Dear Abby" column is syndicated in hundreds of newspapers nationwide. When her sister did a little soul searching of her own some years ago, asking for advice on whether her column was still in demand, thousands of her readers insisted that she continue. Only one reader urged her to stop; she signed herself "Abby."

The man responsible for "arranging" the Nixon-Khrushchev "kitchen debate" in which Nixon put the Soviet premier "in his place" was *William Safire* (1929–   ). This incident catapulted Nixon into the international arena. Safire, who subsequently wrote foreign policy speeches for Nixon, was said to be "the word factory's resident pro for zingers and snappers."

Tall, blue-eyed, slouchy, and raspy voiced, Safire began writing for the *New York Times* in 1973. His op-ed articles appear twice weekly and invariably arouse deep emotions pro and con. He also composes a weekly "On Language" column for the *New York Times Magazine,* which is syndicated to nearly four hundred newspapers.

When asked how he can handle such diverse subjects, he replies, "It's a welcome relief to turn from a go-for-the-jugular political column to a go-for-the-funnybone or go-for-the-brain column."

A friend attended the opening night of a play in the winter of 1949. He told me that when the final curtain went down there was silence. Not a soul in the theatre found the strength to move. Then the applause began, at first a trickle, then a thundering ovation, until the tall, emaciated-looking man walked onstage to acknowledge his sudden fame.

Arthur Miller (1915–   ), thirty-four when he wrote *Death of a Salesman,* modeled Willy Loman, a pathetic figure, after his boastful salesmen uncles who were frequent visitors to his family's Brooklyn home.

The son of a coat manufacturer, Miller was a poor student. He confessed that "until the age of seventeen I can safely say that I never read a book weightier than *Tom Swift* and *The Rover Boys*." Miller began to write at the University of Michigan, winning several awards.

For a time he turned out radio scripts and finally had a play produced on Broadway. It closed after four performances. Three years later *All My Sons* won the New York Drama Critics Circle Award. Later hits, including *The Crucible* and *A View from the Bridge,* earned him the reputation of a major American dramatist.

Considered one of the most brilliant and successful "British" playwrights, *Tom Stoppard* (1937–   ) was born in Czechoslovakia, the second son of Dr. Eugene and Martha Straussler. Forced to flee from the invading Nazis, the family settled in Singapore, only to be evacuated again, this time to India, just prior to the Japanese occupation. Dr. Straussler stayed behind and was murdered.

While in India, Mrs. Straussler married a British Army officer, Kenneth Stoppard—young Tom adopted his name. The Stoppard family later settled in Bristol, England, where Tom completed his education.

Starting as a journalist and then gaining experience as a drama critic, Stoppard wrote his first play, *A Walk on the Water,* which was produced on British television in 1963. His complicated plots and provocative dialogue have fascinated playgoers ever since. At this moment, tickets are hard to get for *The Real Thing* which has played in London and New York for several years.

Clive Barnes notes that Stoppard "plays with ideas like a juggler—sharp, clear and dazzling. . . . He sees the theatre as a kind of trampoline for the intellect, a sauna bath for the mind. It is all very refreshing."

As for Stoppard himself, he confesses that he is "lazy."

In his play *Artist Descending a Staircase,* a character pro-
claims that, out of one thousand people, nine hundred will
be "doing the work," ninety will be "doing well," nine will
be "doing good," and one lucky guy will be "writing about
the other nine hundred and ninety-nine."

Creator of L'il Abner, Daisy Mae, Mammy and Pappy
Yokum, and other celebrated Dogpatch characters, cartoon-
ist-satirist *Al Capp* (1909–1979) (Caplin) invented an American comic-strip mythology that remains as relevant to our
lives today as when Capp first started drawing profession-
ally over fifty years ago.

In his early teens, Capp ran away from his Connecticut
home and found himself in the Cumberland Mountains.
From that brief experience he invented Dogpatch, which
has so fascinated his wide readership that for years students
have celebrated "Sadie Hawkins Day," the day in Dogpatch
when a man must marry the first woman who catches him.

Writer Emily Hahn said of him, "Al Capp in my esti-
mation is just about the most wonderful man we have today
in the world of entertainment, maybe outside that world as
well. His drawing, excellent as it is, is only secondary to
his stories and his little extra touches and his fantastic,
completely goofy brain."

Al Capp left the world a rare legacy of humor.

Among the most civic minded publishers in America,
Katherine Graham (1917–   ) is a trustee of the University of Chicago, George Washington University, Columbia
University, and St. Alban's School. She graces the advisory
committee to the Kennedy School of Government, the Ad-
vertising Council, Business Committee for the Arts, the
Committee for Economic Development, and others.

The daughter of banker Eugene Meyer, she puts in a full
schedule as publisher of the *Washington Post,* which, in

turn, controls *Newsweek*, one of the nation's largest weekly magazines.

Occasionally, the efforts of playwrights or authors were crowned with a prize named after *Joseph Pulitzer* (1847–1911). Pulitzer is remembered today not only as a remarkable figure in American journalism, but also as the founder and developer of Columbia University's School of Journalism and the Pulitzer Prizes "for the encouragement of public service, public morals, American literature and the advancement of education."

EPILOGUE

Christians revere the Jewish Jesus but incongruously have been conditioned to denigrate his people—a reaction to Gospel accounts of Jesus' crucifixion.

Is this implication to be accepted literally? Do we give credence to the flat statement from the Hebrew Scriptures that the world was created 4,000 years ago in seven days?

The precise events leading to Jesus' death are enshrouded in the mists of two millennia. We do know that Gospel compilers Mark, Matthew, and John were Jewish. Would they deliberately condemn their brethren to a future of torture and repression? Moreover, it is known that five million Jews, by far the majority, lived *outside Palestine*. A considerably smaller group existed under Roman oppression in what is now Israel. Far from rejecting Jesus, all who experienced his magnetic presence were entranced by him. His Jewish followers, later made saints by the Church, believed that he was the Messiah.

Authoritative theologians have pointed out that references to "the Jews" should not be interpreted as accurate history but rather as a vehicle to remove the new religion from the synagogue where it had begun as a Judaic/Christian sect decades before.

Now, almost twenty centuries after Jesus' birth, enlightened Protestant, Catholic, and Orthodox church leaders are

144

rejecting certain interpretations of biblical teachings as the basis for anti-Semitism. They recognize that Christianity has no need to degrade any other religion in order to validate itself. They counsel that to be a good Christian religious, political, and racial intolerance must be repudiated.

There are many practical reasons now to strip away superstition and age-old myths. Our lives are already shadowed by the reality of underemployment, crime, and family instability in our communities. Abroad, our shared universe is threatened by terrorism, uncontrolled population growth and food shortages in poorer countries, and an ever-present menace of nuclear accident.

These are real problems that demand the brain power, judgment, and dedication of *all* citizens of our composite society. People, not oil or coal, are the nation's greatest resource.

Musicians, artists, and entertainers are ambassadors of good will throughout the world. Gifted scientists, medical pioneers, and public servants have lengthened our life span and helped preserve our mutually cherished institutions.

To waste these human assets because of differences in how we pray to the same God is contrary to the most fundamental American precepts.

Transforming fresh knowledge into positive action is a measure of true Christian ecumenism. Adults can play an important role in developing new values for younger generations, helping them to discard stereotypes, providing guidance in exploring the common roots of Christianity and Judaism, stressing particularly Jesus' Jewish heritage. With this knowledge, young people can be better prepared to reject bigotry.

Jesus was beloved by his people. In our time, many of the same faith labor in a similar tradition on behalf of the community and of all humanity. For every discerning Christian, there is a Jesus connection and a Jewish connection. They are interrelated.

LAST WORDS

33:12 Blessed is the nation whose God is
       the Lord,
       the people he chose for his
       inheritance.
33:13 From heaven the Lord looks down
       and sees all mankind.
33:14 from his dwelling place he watches
       all who live on earth—
33:15 he who forms the hearts of all,
       who considers everything they do.
33:16 No king is saved by the size of his
       army:
       no warrior excapes by his great
       strength.
33:17 A horse is a vain hope for
       deliverance;
       despite all its great strength it
       cannot save.
33:18 But the eyes of the Lord are on those
       who fear him,
       on those whose hope is in his
       unfailing love,

33:19 to deliver them from death
        and keep them alive in famine.

33:20 We wait in hope for the Lord;
        he is our help and our shield.

33:21 In him our hearts rejoice,
        for we trust in his holy name.

33:22 May your unfailing love rest upon us,
          O Lord,
        even as we put our hope in you.

◆FROM THE PROVERBS OF SOLOMON ◆

3:27   Do not withhold good from those
         who deserve it,
      when it is in your power to act.
3:29   Do not plot harm against your
         neighbor,
      who lives trustfully near you.
3:30   Do not accuse a man for no reason—
      when he has done you no harm.
4:14   Do not set foot on the path of the
         wicked
      or walk in the way of evil men.
4:15   Avoid it, do not travel on it;
      turn from it and go on your way.
4:16   For they cannot sleep till they do evil;
      they are robbed of slumber till they
         make someone fall.
4:17   They eat the bread of wickedness
      and drink the wine of violence,
4:18   The path of the righteous is like the
         first gleam of dawn,
      shining ever brighter till the full
         light of day.
5:12   Hatred stirs up dissension,
         but love covers over all wrongs.
5:17   He who heeds discipline shows the
         way to life,
      but whoever ignores correction
         leads others astray.

PICTURE CREDITS

American Jewish Archives, Cincinnati Campus, Hebrew Union College Jewish Institute of Religion
Mike Goldwater, Rebecca Gratz

A/P Wide World Photos
Ed Asner, Lauren Bacall, Bernard Baruch, Jack Benny, Herbert L. Block, Margaret Bourke-White, Joyce Brothers, Harold Brown, Arthur Burns, Dyan Cannon, Joan Collins, Howard Cosell, Jamie Lee Curtis, Tony Curtis, Marcel Dessault, Kirk Douglas, Bob Dylan, Erik Erikson, Dianne Feinstein with Pope John Paul II, Arthur Fiedler, Paul Michael Glaser, Katherine Graham, Cary Grant, Lorne Greene, Ernest Gruening, Goldie Hawn, Joseph Heller, John Houseman, Jacob Javits, Billy Joel, Danny Kaye, Jerome Kern, Henry Kissinger, Jack Klugman, Ted Koppel, Arthur Kornberg, Edwin Land, Ann Landers, Michael Landon, Joshua Lederberg, Herbert Lehman, Barry Manilow, Albert A. Michelson, Louise Nevelson, Edwin Newman, Mike Nichols, William S. Paley, Tony Randall, Abraham Ribicoff, Hyman Rickover, William Safire, David Sarnoff, Scene from *Porgy and Bess*, George Segal, William Shatner, Jill St. John, Rod Steiger, Gloria Steinem, Tom Stoppard, Rosalyn Sussman Yalow, Gerard Swope, Abigail van Buren, Barbara Walters, Norbert Wiener, Jerome Wiesner, Debra Winger, Henry Winkler, Shelley Winters

Avco Embassy Pictures Corp.
Dustin Hoffman, from the motion picture *The Graduate*. Copyright © 1967.

Elliot Caplan
Al Capp: © Capp Enterprises 1985.

Collections of the Library of Congress
Emile Berliner, Leonard Bernstein, Claude C. Bloch, Louis D. Brandeis, Benjamin N. Cardozo, Andre Citroën, Thomas A. Edison, Douglas Fairbanks, Sr., Harvey S.

Firestone, Felix Frankfurter, Vladimir Horowitz, Thomas Lipton, Dorothy Parker, Joseph Pulitzer, Julius Rosenwald

Culver Pictures
August Belmont, Victor Borge, Melvyn Douglas and Sylvia Sydney, Eddie Duchin, Albert Einstein, Sigmund Freud, Paulette Goddard, Lillian Hellman, Judy Holliday, Leslie Howard, Fiorello LaGuardia, Arthur Miller, Paul Newman, Edward G. Robinson, Jonas Salk, Peter Sellers, Charles P. Steinmetz, Mike Wallace

Jan Howarth, Aspen, Colorado
Beverly Sills

International Museum of Photography at George Eastman House
George Gershwin

Movie Star News
George Burns with Gracie Allen

Musée: Orsay - Jeu de Paume
Camille Pissarro

The Museum of Modern Art, New York
Chaim Soutine, *Chartes Cathedral* (1933). Oil on Wood, 36 x 19³/₄". Collection, The Museum of Modern Art, New York. Gift of Mrs. Lloyd Bruce Wescott.

Ullstein Bilderdienst
Marc Chagall

UPI/Bettman Newsphoto
Gene Barry, Saul Bellow with King Gustav of Sweden, Mr. and Mrs. Irving Berlin with President Eisenhower, Art Buchwald, James Caan and Barbra Streisand, Paul Ehrlich, Peter Falk, Bonnie Franklin, David Janssen, Madeline Kahn, Linda Lavin, Hal Linden, Werner Klemperer, Amedeo Modigliani, I.I. Rabi, Luise Rainer and Paul Muni, Dinah Shore, August von Wassermann, Selman A. Waksman, Theodore H. White

INDEX

Anderson, Broncho Billy, 109
Asner, Ed, 117

Bacall, Lauren, 86, 115
Bacon, Francis, 11
Baker, Samuel, 79
Bara, Theda, 109
Barbie, Klaus, 15
Barnes, Albert, 135
Baruch, Bernard, 90, 100, 101
Bell, Alexander Graham, 94
Bellow, Saul, 136
Belmont, August, 98
Benchley, Robert, 139
Bennett, Constance, 114
Benny, Jack, 124
Berlin, Irving, 128
Berliner, Emile, 94
Bernardin, Cardinal Joseph, 67
Bernstein, Elias, 65
Bernstein, Leonard, 128, 129
Billot, General, 51
Bloch, Claude C., 102
Blumenthal, Ferdinand, 60
Bogart, Humphrey, 115
Bobl, Dr., 60
Borah, William, 100
Borge, Victor, 130
Boschwitz, Rudy, 107, 108
Bouyer, Louis, 69
Boyer, Charles, 115
Boxer, Barbara, 106

Bradford, William, 83
Brandeis, Louis, 97, 99, 100
Browder, Earl, 104
Buchwald, Art, 7, 138
Burns, Arthur F., 193
Burns, George, 124

Caan, James, 112
Cannon, Dyan, 116, 117
Capote, Truman, 126
Capp, Al, 142
Cardozo, Benjamin, 97, 100
Carter, Jimmy, 104
Cassatt, Mary, 133
Chagall, Marc, 133
Churchill, Winston, 123
Cleaver, Eldridge, 126
Clemenceau, Georges, 50
Clift, Montgomery, 112
Cohen, Mickey, 126
Colbert, Claudette, 114
Collins, Joan, 121
Constantine, 46
Cooper, Gary, 115
Cosell, Howard, 125
Crassus, Marcus Licinus, 36
Crawford, Broderick, 111
Curie, Madame, 90

Darrow, Clarence, 59
Davis, Bette, 111
Day, Doris, 120

de Boisdeffre, General, 49
Dine, Jim, 132
Dineen, Madge, vi
Diva, Maria, 122
Douglas, Kirk, 7, 86, 110, 115
Douglas, Melvyn, 113
Dorsey, Peter, 75
Dreyfus, Captain Alfred, 48, 49, 51, 52, 54
Duchin, Eddie, 86, 130
du Paty de Clam, Colonel, 51
Dulles, John Foster, 101
Dylan, Bob, 86, 130

Eichmann, Adolf, 57
Einstein, Albert, 7, 88
Eisenhower, Dwight D., 103
Erikson, Erik H., 91
Esterhazy, Major Marie C.F.W., 48, 49, 51
Etchegaray, Cardinal Roger, 67
Eustis, Warren, 74

Fairbanks, Sr., Douglas, 87, 109
Fahlberg, Constantine, 84
Falk, Peter, 122
Faure, Felix, 51
Feinstein, Dianne, 108
Ferber, Edna, 128
Fiedler, Arthur, 86, 131
Filehne, Dr., 59
Flannery, Rev. Edward H., 30, 67
Forrestal, James, 101
Foster, Stephen, 86
France, Anatole, 53
Frankenthaler, Helen, 132
Frankfurter, Felix, 97, 99
Frankl, Oscar, 60
Freud, Sigmund, 59, 88

Garbo, Greta, 114
Gauguin, Eugene Henri Paul, 134
Gershwin, George, 128
Gessius Florus, 41
Goddard, Paulette, 86
Goldwater, Barry, 97, 98
Goldwater, "Big Mike," 98
Gonse, General, 49
Gottlieb, Adolph, 132

Graham, Katherine, 142
Graham, Billy, 67
Grant, Cary, 87
Green, Julian, 70
Greene, Lorne, 86
Gruening, Ernest, 102

Halasz, Nicholas, 53
Hamilton, Alexander, 86
Hammerstein, Oscar, 129
Hardon, Rev. John A., 33
Hart, Moss, 86, 144
Hawks, Howard, 115
Hawn, Goldie, 113
Hays, Jacob, 97
Hays, John, 97
Heller, Joseph, 136
Heller, Samuel, 75
Hellman, Lillian, 136, 137, 139
Hesburgh, Rev. Theodore, 2, 67
Hitler, Adolf, 4, 55, 58
Hoess, Rudolph, 56
Holliday, Judy, 111
Holmes, John Haynes, 7
Holmes, Oliver Wendell, 64
Hoover, Herbert, 100
Hope, Bob, 124
Horowitz, Vladimir, 11, 12, 130
Houseman, John, 123
Howard, Leslie, 109
Hudson, Rock, 120

Jabot, Archbishop Jean, 67
Janssen, David, 122, 123
Javits, Jacob, 97
Jefferson, Thomas, 13, 97
Joan of Arc, 55
Joel, Billy, 86, 130
John Chrysostom, St., 4
John XXIII, Pope, 61, 62, 63

Kaufman, George S., 139
Kaye, Danny, 114, 115
Kean, Governor Thomas, 66
Kennedy, John F., 37
Kennedy, Robert, 37
Kern, Jerome, 128
Kerr, Walter, 118
Kitchener, Lord, 54

Kissinger, Henry, 97, 104
Kline, Franz, 132
Klugman, Jack, 120
Koppel, Edward James, 123
Kornberg, Arthur, 89

LaGuardia, Fiorello, 87, 92, 98
Land, Edwin, 92
Landers, Ann, 139
Landon, Michael, 87
Lantos, Tom, 107
Lawrence, Gertrude, 114
Lederberg, Joshua, 91
Lehman, Herbert H., 97
Lemmon, Jack, 111
Libo, Kenneth, vi
Lichtenstein, Roy, 132
Liebreich, Oscar, 59
Lincoln, Abraham, 75, 99
Loring, Lynn, 121

Madison, James, 97
Manet, Edouard, 134
Marino, Bishop Eugene, 67
Martin, Malachi, 34, 35
Maslin, Janet, 113
May, Elaine, 118
McDowell, Roddy, 122
McGarry, Ann, 138
Mendelsohn, Felix, 128
Mercier, General, 51
Metzenbaum, Howard, 105
Meyer, Eugene, 142
Meyerbeer, Giacomo, 128
Michelson, Albert, 95
Milk, Harvey, 108
Miller, Arthur, 136, 140
Minkowski, Dr., 59
Mitchell, John, 126
Modigliani, Amedeo, 133, 134
Monet, Claude, 134
Moore, Bishop Paul, 67, 68
Monroe, Marilyn, 86
Moscone, George, 108
Muggeridge, Malcolm, 47
Murrow, Edward R., 101

Napoleon III, 134
Neisser, Dr., 59

Newman, Paul, 86, 111
Neumann, Heinrich, 59
Nero, 42
Nevelson, Louise, 132
Nichols, Mike, 118
Nicholson, Jack, 113
Nimoy, Leonard, 119
Nixon, Richard, 103, 140
Noah, Mordecai Manuel, 97
Nones, Benjamin, 97

Oberon, Merle, 114
O'Brien, Howard Vincent, 59
O'Casey, Sean, 82
Offenbach, Jacques, 128
Olsen, Bernhard E., 34
Olson, Arnold Theodore, 85
O'Malley, Sean, 77
Ormondy, Eugene, 86
Osler, Sir William, 58

Paley, William S., 101, 102
Pappas, Rev. Arthur N., 72
Parker, Dorothy, 136, 137, 139
Patterson, Robert, 101
Paul of Tarsus, 39, 40
Pawlikowski, John T., 14
Peck, Gregory, 115
Pellieux, General, 52
Perry, Caroline, 98
Perry, Commodore, 98
Pickford, Mary, 109
Picquart, Colonel, 49
Pissarro, Camille, 133
Pliny the Younger, 43
Pulitzer, Joseph, 143

Randall, Tony, 120
Ratner, Abraham, 132
Ravary, Major, 52
Redford, Robert, 86
Renoir, Pierre Auguste, 134
Ribicoff, Abraham, 97, 103
Rickover, Hyman, 92
Rockefeller, Nelson A., 104
Rodgers, Richard, 86, 129
Roncalli, Monsignor Angelo, (Pope
   John XXIII)
Roosevelt, Franklin D., 92, 99, 101

Rosenwald, Julius, 75, 76
Ross, Harold, 139
Russell, Rosalind, 114
Safire, William, 136, 140
Salk, Jonas, 87, 88, 90
Salomon, Haym, 97
Sargent, Winthrop, 129
Sarnoff, David, 93, 94
Schlatter, George, 113
Schrift, Johan, 112
Schwertfeger, Colonel, 54
Segal, George, 132
Sellers, Peter, 116
Seurat, Georges, 134
Shahn, Ben, 132
Shakespeare, William, 134
Shatner, William, 86, 119
Shirer, William L., 101
Shore, Dinah, 86, 128
Sichel, Pierre, 134
Sills, Beverly, 129
Simond, Gilbert, 62
Sisley, 134
Smith, Howard K., 101
Soutine, Chaim, 132, 135
Spartacus, 36
Spiegelman, Solomon, 91
Spiro, Dr., 59
Spong, Bishop John Selby, 29, 84
Stanwyck, Barbara, 114
Stein, Gertrude, 123
Steinmetz, Charles, 96
Stimson, Henry L., 99
Stoppard, Tom, 141
Stricker, Solomon, 59
Suetonius, 43
Swanson, Gloria, 11
Swope, Gerard, 85

Tacitus, 36
Taft, Robert, 105
Taft, William Howard, 99

Tanenbaum, Rabbi Marc, vi, 67
Taylor, Elizabeth, 112
Thiering, Sister Rose, 67
Thomson, Virgil, 123
Trajan, 43, 44
Traube, Ludwig, 59
Truman, Harry S., 101
Twain, Mark, 52

Van Buren, Abigail, 139
Vidal, Gore, 112
von Schwartzkoppen, Colonel Max, 48, 54
von Schwartzkoppen, Louise, 54

Waksman, Selman A., 89
Wallace, Mike, 126
Walters, Barbara, 126
Warner, Jack, 115
Washington, George, 13
Wassermann, August von, 59
Wayne, John, 110
Weil, Dr., 59
Weissmuller, Johnny, 122
Welles, Orson, 123
White, Theodore, 136, 137, 138
Widal, Dr., 59
Weiner, Norbert, 96
Williams, Roger, 14
Wilson, Woodrow, 99, 101
Windsor, Duke of, 66
Winger, Debra, 113
Winkler, Henry, 119
Winters, Shelley, 112
Winward, Estelle, 112
Woollcott, Alexander, 139

Yalow, Rosalyn, 90
Yaseen, Helen, vi

Zola, Emile, 51, 52, 53
Zorinsky, Edward, 106